Wounds to Wisdom

Fear to Financial Freedom

Wounds to Wisdom

Fear to Financial Freedom

by Orane Swan

"A pearl is a beautiful thing that is produced by an injured life. It is the tear that results from the injury of the oyster. The treasure of our being in this world is also produced by an injured life. If we had not been wounded, if we had not been injured, then we will not produce the pearl." Stephen Hoeller

Copyright © 2013 Orane Swan

Cover designed by Orane Swan

Cover image by Joshua Swan

Title page image © Africa Studio - Fotolia.com

ISBN: 978-0-99231-040-0
ISBN: 978-0-99231-041-7 (ebook)

All rights reserved. No part of this publication may be reproduced in any form or by any electronic or mechanical means, including information storage or retrieval systems, without permission in writing from the author, except by a reviewer who may quote brief passages.

Requests for permission should be sent to admin@keepingontrack.com.au.

Visit Orane on the internet at
www.keepingontrack.com.au.

DISCLAIMER
This book contains the concepts and insights of its author and reflects on their own results and transformation. The strategies employed and shared by the author may not be appropriate for everybody, they are not guaranteed to produce any specific results and they are not intended to replace professional counselling.

The author and publisher assume no responsibility for any errors, omissions, or contrary interpretation of the subject matter. The author and publisher assume no responsibility or liability for any loss, injury or damage allegedly arising from any information or suggestions in this book.

Preface

"Only when you accept that one day you'll die can you let go, and make the best out of life. And that's the big secret. That's the miracle."

Gabriel Bá

I reminisce the past and remember the days as a single parent of four children: having to balance work and home, the days of chaotic mornings whisking the kids into my beaten up Datsun 120Y which would not even start most mornings, trying to get the kids to school on time and getting in trouble again for arriving three minutes late for work. After a hard day at work, I would rush home through the heavy traffic, exhausted. I would arrive home after a long day with hungry children to feed, only to find the electricity switched off as I had ignored the three overdue electricity notices. Not again, I would think to myself. I even had a debt collector knock on my front door one evening to serve the papers to repossess the home I had worked so hard to provide for my family. These were the TOUGH years. I wish that I had known then that life could be different by making some different choices.

Today, my life is transformed from that of yesterday: I am no longer shackled to a job, I have become my own master and created my key to financial freedom. I rise in the morning and make my own decisions as to whether I choose to work or not, I decide my own pay cheque. I decide my own hours and I sleep late if I choose to do so. I choose whether I go to the gym or have a massage. I have planned for my future and my money will give me more dignity in old age. Against the odds, I decided to trust my intuition and take risks and through following the steps of **CONFIDENCE, CLARITY, CHOICE, CREATIVITY, COMMUNICATION, COLLABORATION** and **CASHFLOW**, I now own an array of residential, commercial, retail and development sites throughout Brisbane. My property portfolio returns more money and satisfaction in a year than I would earn working for ten years shackled to the average 9 to 5 job as I did in my former life. My money works for me 24/7 instead of me having to work for money.

I have just returned from a world trip, where I admired the architecture of Rome, the Taj Mahal in India and the pyramids of Egypt. I absorbed the picturesque scenery of Florence and the magnificence of Dubai. I indulged in fine cuisine in Barcelona and even raised a glass of champagne at the recent Cannes film festival in France.

For the first time in my life, I am truly happy and content, the chaos of my life has been replaced with a sense of calm and I am no longer addicted to misery. I live in gratitude for every breath I take. I try to live each moment without fear of my past or the anxiety of the future. I have learnt to tame my emotions as I have developed a sense of self-mastery; I am now able to withstand the emotional storm that once debilitated me.

I started writing this book in 2003. It was one of these things that I would drift back to periodically but never really dedicated the time to completing. I returned to my writing a few days after my brother passed away in 2012. His passing brought me in touch with my own mortality and reignited my obsessive fear of death. It made me realise that while our physical body may want specific things, our souls may need something altogether different. This power struggle that rages within each of us creates inner tension and sorrow. At fifty, I thought I had everything, but the passing of my brother brought me face to face with the orphan inside me that needed more.

I have written this book as a contribution to people similar to myself, who have had to struggle throughout their life to make friends with their inner being and peace with the world outside. My message to other sufferers of depression is that there is help and there is hope. If you are finding the road difficult, take another step forward and reach out for help. You too can buy your own freedom. The cost is not high, yet it seems high to those who don't have the courage to pay the price. What is the price? You must be willing to be the master of your mind and not its slave. You must become a master in emotional and financial intelligence.

Acknowledgements

To my children, Benjamin, Matthew, Joshua and Jessica. You were the wind beneath my wings. I love you.

To my Mother, for your heart which can do nothing by itself if it is not loved. You left the safety of your country so that your children could have a better life. So many times, you went without and gave to us instead. You made me feel that I belonged, that I was part of a large family. For my passion in cooking, I learnt from the best.

To my Father, thank you for my entrepreneurial creative and my risk-taking mind which led to my financial success and my redemption. I never had mentors in property but always knew what to do and trusted my intuition. I knew you were watching over me from above. I did not get to tell you I loved you before you died.

To my sister Marie, thank you for your financial help when I had debt collectors knocking on my door. Thank you for taking my children away for six months to give me time to recuperate. You have been a pillar of strength in my life and the lives of my children. I thank you for the many books you have given me since I was 16 years old. I am proud and honoured to have you as my sister, my friend and my spiritual mentor. I love you.

To Marissa, my best friend for the past 30 years. You have seen me at my best; you have seen me at my worst. You have helped me through the dark night of the soul on many occasions. I thank you.

To my business partner and lawyer, Bryan, thank you for your support and your legal advice. Thank you for your continued contribution to my life, you were a pillar of strength and helped me through the GFC, you saved me.

To my ex-husband, I forgive you for leaving me. My wounds now that they are healed are precious to me; they have carved in me wisdom that I cherish.

To Alan, Peter, Walter and Steve, thank you for your contribution to my life.

To Lilly, I thank you for being instrumental in encouraging me to change my life into something more fulfilling.

To Anne Maree, I thank you for encouraging me to publish my story.

To Lorraine Smith, my editor from Proof Edit Me, who has been a pillar of strength to me the past months. Thank you for believing in me, encouraging me and for your unconditional support.

"Once you know who you are, where you are going, how you are going to get there and what you are prepared to lose to get what you want, nothing can stop you."

Orane Swan

This is the story of two swans, one black and one white. One morning after a restless night, I approached my spiritual master and confessed.

"Master, it is like there are two swans battling for command of my heart. The black swan characterises the yearnings for pain and negativity, while the white swan exemplifies pleasure and the desire to succeed. The black swan longs for darkness, while the white swan shines comfortably in the light. Both swans are of equal strength. The struggle that rages in my heart is severe, for choosing one means losing the other. I am afraid that it could go either way for they are both beneficial to me. The black, the secular, and the white, the Soul. Like a seesaw, the black and white swans equally attempt to outweigh each other. Tell me master, which one will win?"

*With a sparkle of acknowledgment in his eyes, the master calmly responded, "You will know, because the swan that will win is the swan that you **feed the most**".*

Part 1

The struggle

"The worst loneliness is not to be comfortable with yourself."

Mark Twain

These words clatter around my head during a turbulent flight back from Launceston. I sit motionless, staring out of the window, trying to avert my attention from my own reflection to focus on the misty void beyond. As I stare at the nothingness from inside the plane, I feel an overwhelming sense of loss and I wonder how much more I can endure. Loss is a strange word. It can mean a lot or it can mean very little. I'm not sure exactly what I've lost, but it is some part of my soul that just isn't there for me—perhaps it never was. I feel emptiness where I know there should be something important, but I don't know what it is or how to find it. The darkness in my soul continues to strangle my being as it has for as long as I can remember. It is depression and it swallows me whole. It hovers, like the metaphoric 'black dog', ready to pounce whenever the atmosphere is ripe and my soul is there for the picking.

My life has been like this turbulent ride, bumpy to say the least. Sitting here, I realise that I have lived a self-condemning life, full of feelings of misery, confusion and despair. I snap at people. I have become professionally aggressive and competitive to the point of being confrontational. Each day I push myself to exhaustion. Why do I do it? Simply put, because over the years I have found stress to be invigorating. It energises me and makes me feel alive; it motivates me to achieve. The adrenalin rush is addictive and it's what I have come to need in order to succeed. Stress is my security blanket.

Eventually the turbulence becomes calming in its own weird way. As the plane bumps around in the misty sky, I think of how we as humans travel through life from the cradle to the grave. I think about the roads we can choose to navigate on this journey and what that choice will mean to each of us in the end. What have my choices meant for me? As I sit there transfixed on the nothingness outside, I know in my mind there is a road of confidence and control that provides calmness and contentment to its travellers. A fleeting feeling of unease ripples through me and I reluctantly acknowledge the road I know is mine; one of competition and combat that leaves me battered, with chaos and conflict as my guideposts. I try hard to think about why I have chosen the latter. I look at my reflection in the window and the disconnection with that image staring back at me is disturbing. It is the image of a companion traveller but I don't really know who she is or where she is going. I try to focus again on the distance as if there is something out there for me, if only I could grab hold of it.

The state of madness I choose to drive me forward in life manifests itself in a cold shiver and I pull the blanket more tightly around me. I think about the contrasting faces of this madness; the way they cleverly disguise themselves as motivation, success and confidence. And it works. Insanity does get results, but they are never good enough and so the cycle reproduces itself repeatedly until the 'black dog' finds its weary way home. Insanity is my constant ally. It has served many purposes and never failed to deliver. When I was in a dysfunctional co-dependent relationship, I felt I would go insane if it ended. It did, and I did.

From madness, my mind drifts towards anger, a natural progression. The void beyond the window is filled by images of my past. I recall many times when I had been angry with my mother, resented my brothers and sisters and mad at myself because I so badly wanted to control everything and everyone but never could. Even though I was always surrounded by people, I was constantly lonely and never felt happy. It seems like misery is the veil through which I view my past; it is my heritage and part of my subconscious.

My anger begins to turn inward, as anger always does eventually. I feel like I have been a horrible mother, dragging my children through the dark alleys of depression I seem to have travelled so frequently and so willingly. I know those alleys. I know all the twists and turns, the potholes and the occasional glimmers in the distance that prove_–to be no more than a phantom light.

I know that the only escape from that darkness were those fractures in time when my other addiction, work, vied for control. Those were the times I would rouse myself and run from the darkness towards a new goal. I ran swiftly because I was running from myself and didn't want to be caught. I was running to be successful; running to make it better for my children and running to make up for lost time. My obsession for making money engulfed my thoughts and actions. The darkness of inactivity was rapidly replaced by the light of my growing financial success. Making money made me happy. It made me less angry and I felt the chaos dissipate to make way for the calm. I could see into the distance and the road ahead beckoned me with its promise of success and wealth.

During those times of hyperactivity and increased wealth, an intensified self-awareness and self-confidence developed, and my success grew exponentially. While the zeal to really transform my life would take root in my subconscious there were still many battles fought between old foes. Like sibling twins, chaos and misery were always waiting in the wings ready to take flight and spread their darkness over my soul yet again. And they always found their chance to make their mark.

As I sit on the plane, I shake my head and try to think past the density of the dark that impaired my vision so completely for so long. I am no longer in the clutches of that darkness. I'm transformed. I'm successful. I have made it. I have a huge property portfolio, passive income, financial independence, a Mercedes convertible, a waterfront home; I have everything I need to be happy and secure. I am far away from the poverty I rubbed shoulders with as a child. I don't have to fear being old and poor. I now rub shoulders with other 'success stories'. I have taken care of it all.

But have I? Today, sitting here in this plane, unable to move and forced to think, I can sense the presence of that old 'black dog' gnawing at my insides; leaving an empty cavern that I know I can't fill. I fear that feeling because I know what it can lead to. It can toss me around in its turbulence leaving me feeling unfulfilled, unsettled and unstable. This is the feeling that causes me to turn things upside down, looking for the answer somewhere else, with someone else or through something else. I've given this feeling a name—it's Fear of Failure. Sometimes during a bad night, I can almost reach out and touch Fear of Failure. It has a face; a medley of the old homeless people I was once familiar with in my homeland. It has a smell; the smell of the alleyways where the homeless cooked, ate and slept and the stench of sewage and rubbish mingled with them so they smelt one and the same. It has a feeling, a feeling that grabs me by the throat and tries to strangle me. Fear of Failure robs me of everything I have. It takes me on a wild goose chase to find what it is that I don't have. Fear of Failure does not manifest as beauty or houses or family. It's not even happiness because I think I have that. What is Failure—really?

I close my eyes momentarily then open them and try to refocus. I realise that most of my life I have searched for happiness outside of myself; through beauty, family, possessions, relationships, marriage and love, but I am yet to find real happiness. The feeling of happiness that I believe sits comfortably deep inside a person, not just a feeling but a knowing.

The plane is getting lower in the sky. I can see the lights below and try to pull myself back to life. Life! The word sticks in my head and I say it over and over. We touch down and I know instinctively that I need to change my life. I need to stop running and start finding out how to live. I know it, but how will I do it?

Part 2

Finding the courage to change

"Success is not final, failure is not fatal: it is the courage to continue that counts."

Winston Churchill

So, who am I? Who is Orane, the woman staring out of the window trying to avoid that ghostly image superimposed on the empty evening sky?

This I know. I was born on the small island of Mauritius. An island just forty-five kilometres wide and sixty-five kilometres long; located two thousand kilometres from the south east coast of Africa and to the east of Madagascar. It is a tropical island of such beauty that it prompted Mark Twain to write:

"You gather the idea that Mauritius was made first, then heaven, and that heaven was copied after Mauritius."

The island is a vibrant blend of diversity set in a kaleidoscope of tropical colours, sounds and scents. These sounds come back to me now, as real as when I was a child, from the sounds of the sea during all its different moods to the sound of the wind rushing through the fully-grown sugar cane.

Those special feelings that are Mauritius flow through me at a subconscious level. Sometimes just the smell of a spice or a meal that connects to my childhood and family life bring those years flooding back and I find myself thinking the thoughts of long ago.

Mauritius is a culturally diverse mixture of ethnic groups that somehow found their way to this small island. They are represented by differences in religion, dress, language and appearance, but nowhere is this diversity more evident than in Mauritian food. Mauritian food is indeed heaven and my mother was an angel of the kitchen. With a plethora of spices, tropical fruits and exotic herbs, Mauritius provided the canvas for an ethnically diverse culinary art to evolve uninhibited; and it did. I spent many hours in the kitchen with my mother and learnt from her how to master the best of Mauritian cuisine. Mauritian food is a medley of different colours, textures and tastes bound together by technique to create a perfect whole, and my mother mastered the technique beautifully. Mauritians are known for their hospitality and food is an integral component of this cultural mix.

Due to the blend of diverse cultures in my homeland, I learnt to embrace difference and variety early on in life. Poverty and wealth were basic ingredients of life in Mauritius, like the chilli and sugar that provided the basis for many Mauritian dishes. Extreme opposites were accepted as normal; accepted by many on the island as a form of cosmic justice and ratified by whichever religious belief you chose to subscribe to. Ours was Catholicism.

Around the early 1800's, my great grandparents were shipwrecked on the island of Mauritius on their way to Ireland and remained there to become the forbears of my family. My grandmother died when my mother was very young, only three years old, leaving my mother with feelings of abandonment that apparently intensified as she grew towards adulthood, and coloured her responses to the challenges life later threw at her. These circumstances forced her to grow up quickly and take on responsibility at an early age. She matured into a strong looking woman on the outside, but on the inside, she suffered much as the child who had lost her mother prematurely, carrying this hurt with her throughout her life. I was very dependent on my mother for company and only ever felt secure when I was close to her. I was very sensitive to her moods and became anxious if she was unhappy. I spent much of my childhood with her in the kitchen where I watched how she blended the ingredients for the fabulously tasty meals she created.

My mother wanted the best for her large family, but often struggled to provide both materially and emotionally. The relationship between my mother and father was often volatile. My mother was, at times, given to erratic behaviour that saw her disconnect from the family and spend extended periods of time brooding alone in her room. I believe this was the sad result of living in near poverty with an unloving stepmother and alcoholic father. My father compounded my mother's feelings of instability by behaving in a manner common to men of his generation; he was often away from home gambling with friends. This prompted my mother to retreat into a cocoon of hurt and rejection as was evidenced by periods of dysfunctional behaviour.

At a young age, I could not understand why my mother would cut herself off from the rest of the family by retreating into her bedroom. She would emerge many hours later wearing an expression of empty resignation and creating a distance that was difficult for a young child to fathom. This was however, a scenario that later came to be all too familiar as I too grew into a controller of magnificent proportions and developed the ability to throw tantrums that rivalled those of my mother. My mother was an able teacher and I was a willing student.

I have mixed memories of my childhood. I do remember that life was chaotic with frequent emotional outbursts from the people around me. I recall my mother's harshness when giving orders that were to be obeyed at all cost. She saw herself as a righteous woman and was critical in her judgement of others. Her righteousness was evidenced by the frequent visitors to our small home; priests and nuns were a common sight at our dining table and my mother went to great effort to provide them with the best she could afford. Life was ruled by those metaphoric twins of good behaviour; *must* and *should*. I grew up with *must* on one shoulder and *should* on the other and they have tormented me for much of my life. Our home was a somewhat austere place; a reflection of the energy produced by the people that lived within its walls.

Looking back, I realise it was during this time that I somehow felt I was different. I found it almost impossible to concentrate at school and later put it down to the fact that I was constantly worried my mother would kill herself while I was away at school and that I would somehow be to blame. I rushed home every day to save my mother and to feel the security she gave me. My teacher would regularly ridicule me for my inability to learn and I spent many a lunch hour kneeling outside the classroom with the hot sun beating down on my head and a sign on my back validating my academic inadequacies to the whole school. The shame and isolation I felt during those torturously long lunch breaks has returned to haunt me many times during periods of deep depression. This barbaric behaviour from the teacher resulted in teasing from my classmates that eroded any self-esteem I struggled to develop as a child. It goes without saying that I had few friends and found it difficult to relate to other children so, as dysfunctional as my family was for the most part, I always knew that I was loved within its confines and that I belonged to and was accepted by something bigger than myself.

My father on the other hand, was a passive, almost stoic man who showed little emotion. He was largely absent as a parent which left most of the responsibility for the day-to-day management of the family to my mother. He wasn't there physically, but more importantly, he wasn't there for his family emotionally. He did however have two very positive qualities; he was a hard worker and he was entrepreneurial.

During the day, he worked as a health inspector and at night, he would often draw building plans for his clients. Both my mother and father had a passion for property and even sixty years ago and with a large family, would build a house, sell for a small profit, move and repeat the cycle. On the weekends, he made sausages to sell to the neighbours. I guess I could say my father was to some degree a workaholic. Although I don't recall him having a particular presence in our home or having a great influence over my life during these early years, from him I did inherit a respect for hard work and learnt the importance of having multiple streams of income; he taught me the work ethic that has been the cornerstone of my success.

We were a family of eight children of which I was number seven, somewhat low in the pecking order. We lived in a very small, sparse house where siblings always shared a bed as well as other commodities. As Catholics, we were expected to attend church every morning before school and were made to repeat the rosary every evening before going to bed. We lived a highly controlled life, peppered with guilt overlaid by fear; later manifesting as panic attacks through which I developed an obsessive fear of death.

My brothers and sisters were extremely competitive, did well at school and have all become high achievers in their own way, with many of them excelling academically. I, on the other hand, struggled with study all my school life, but managed to harness my competitive streak later in life to make money with property. My financial achievements have really been in response to a vow I made in my early years to never live my life in the kind of poverty I saw all around me in Mauritius. I can vividly remember visiting a hospital when I was about eight years of age and seeing the old and dying living in atrociously poor conditions. Even now, I can see those faces as they looked towards death. Those fleeting encounters with unknown people etched an unforgettable image in my mind and even from that young age, I knew instinctively that money was necessary to provide dignity for my old age.

At this time, Mauritius' economy was still bound to the production of sugar and susceptible to fluctuations in price due to market downturns or natural disaster. Sugar accounted for approximately ninety-nine percent of all export earnings, which left the country vulnerable to sudden changes in economic activity. The cyclones of 1960 that wiped out the sugar crop led to a sixty percent fall in export earnings and is one example of how an economy solely dependent on one source of revenue can be decimated. What I saw at the hospital that day and saw on the streets around me was evidence of such an unsustainable economic strategy. While the population of Mauritius had grown, its economic viability had not. Those images made me determined not to be poor.

In 1967, when I was ten years old, my parents decided to move to Australia. The elections of that year were held amid heightened political upheaval, which eventuated in Mauritius becoming an independent state in 1968. My parents felt that Australia would offer far greater stability and opportunities for the future of their family. Two of my brothers and sisters were the first to leave. They worked very hard when they arrived in Australia and sent money home to help my parents pay for the move. I still have vivid memories of boarding the ship, Australis. I can conjure the smell of the ocean stagnating around the ship and the general sounds of people shuffling on board or saying a final farewell to friends and family. We were strangers connected by a common purpose. My heart felt heavy and light at the same time, as I knew this was a major turning point in our lives.

We spent four weeks at sea before arriving in Sydney, Australia at last!

Walking down from the ship after docking in Australia was, in every way, a rebirthing. Before we even left the docks I could not only see the difference, I could sense it with every fibre of my body. The air smelt different, the people looked different, the language was unintelligible; even the everyday sounds of life were strange. I sensed that change would not be easy.

And I was right. Australia was somewhat less tolerant of immigrants at that time and I suffered my share of prejudice. Unable to speak English, school proved to be a huge challenge. As a child, I wanted so much to fit in but my lack of language skills plus my learning issues made making friends a difficult task. I blamed my heritage for my isolation. I didn't feel that I belonged and didn't know how to change the situation to become accepted by my peers. I was not Australian nor was I Mauritian. I was like a ship without a rudder and I was miserable a lot of the time.

I tried hard to study and learn but the ability to understand and retain information just didn't seem to be there and my situation was not helped in any way by my siblings teasing and calling me 'stupid'. Eventually, I accepted the label and believed I was stupid. Of course, with the acceptance came the associated behaviours and I began to behave in ways that reinforced my lack of self-belief. My feelings of inferiority spurred me on to develop compensatory behaviours and I became increasingly skilled in the art manipulation.

Although I didn't excel academically, I rated highly in terms of my looks, and as I grew older, I found it increasingly easy to use my looks to achieve what I had not been able to achieve by other means. I leveraged my physical attractiveness in ever increasingly sophisticated ways. I began to take work as a model and my sense of self-worth increased, but not in a healthy way. As my main focus in life became my marketable looks, I was increasingly controlled by ego and vanity, which I now see as being equal in effect to the isolation and criticism I experienced as a young child.

Through my late teenage years and into my twenties, life unfolded in a sadly predictable way. My thinking was moulded and dominated by the opinions of other people and the media. I sought acceptance and searched for it through the normal channels of alcohol, music, cigarettes, entertainment and dysfunctional relationships. Life was chaotic but the chaos was useful; it meant I had no time to think clearly or ask questions relating to the meaning and purpose of my life. I felt in control and invincible due to my above average looks and that was all that mattered.

Developing from the little ugly duckling into a swan made a significant change in the way I viewed myself. In spite of my drastic change in lifestyle at my core, I still felt overly controlled by my mother, so at twenty-one, in an effort to attain total freedom over my own life, I married. What I was not capable of understanding at the time was that two half-full people do not make a whole, as they are not able to commit to each other fully. I now understand that it is only when each person knows the depths of their being and are comfortable with what they know that a marriage can truly succeed.

My husband and I had very little in common. He was smart and artistic: a songwriter, poet, guitarist and singer. I on the other hand, was not too smart and felt totally inferior to him. I possessed good looks and was a fabulous cook, but in comparison to him was academically ignorant with a vocabulary that limited the variety and depth of our conversations. I can recall times when his friends would visit and I would hover around the perimeter of the conversations, only contributing when someone commented on the quality of the dinner I had prepared. I could talk about food but little else. My feelings of inadequacy led me to be his intellectual shadow and I carved out a place of secondary importance for myself in our married life. I lived life through his successes and in doing so accepted the fact that he was not able to fulfil my needs emotionally. I remained half-full.

Soon after marriage, I became pregnant with my first son, Benjamin. His birth was truly the highlight of my life. He gave me a sense of purpose that I had never experienced previously. I felt I had finally accomplished something worthwhile and I was as capable of being a mother as anyone else was. Fifteen months later, I gave birth to my second son, Matthew. Six years later, Joshua was born. With these three boys, I experienced most of what there is to know about childbirth. Benjamin was dragged from me after forty-eight hours of labour, Matthew was a natural birth and Joshua was born by caesarean section. My contentment with the role of mother to my three boys effectively papered over the cracks in my marriage for some time. They were my focus and gave me the purpose in life that I felt had been lacking.

My three boys: Matt, Josh and Benjamin

My marriage was essentially quite unstable. We argued over trivial matters and all the while, I unconsciously repeated the behaviour I had learnt from my mother. I too spent a lot of time in my bedroom crying. I became increasingly manipulative and consistently wanted my own way. For many years, I blamed my husband for eventually leaving us. I blamed him for his betrayal in our marriage. Now that I am older and somewhat more enlightened, I can see that I also need to accept responsibility for the demise of our relationship. I have to acknowledge that my low self-esteem, passive aggressive nature and mood swings played a part in the breakdown of our relationship. However, I also have to acknowledge that my husband's behaviour prefaced the episodes of depression that slowly crippled my life.

When I look back now I can identify the strategies that I used to keep myself busy and motivated in the marriage. I may not have been as academically accomplished as my husband and his friends, but one thing I did not feel inadequate about was property. Every Saturday, I would buy the newspaper and scour the property section for likely houses, then call up the agents and pretend I was a potential buyer. I would then look at the houses and discuss the various matters relating to the property and the terms of sale.

At the time, this was my hobby but it proved to be my education also. During my marriage, I was the instigator of all purchases; it was my escape. Although we did buy properties together while married, my husband was risk-averse so buying a property usually proved to be an emotional minefield with the process taking a considerable toll on both of us.

It was before the birth of my second son that I saw a block of land for sale on Coochiemudlo Island in Queensland for $6,000. I desperately wanted to buy it but was afraid of the responsibility so I asked my father to join me in the deal, and he did. Unfortunately, my father had an addiction to gambling which led to us having to sell the land to recoup funds. It was sold a few years later for $16,000. This experience taught me that it was possible to make a considerable amount of money through buying and selling property just by being able to negotiate a deal, buy at the right price and get approval from the bank.

In 1986, I found a block of land for sale at Tarragindi, a suburb of Brisbane in Queensland. I put the profit from the previous block towards this and bought it for $32,000. I reluctantly sold it in 1988 for $60,000. At this point in time, I was a rookie, not an investor. I did what is commonly referred to as flipping—buying and selling for a profit. I lived off the profits I made from buying and selling properties, allowing me to stay at home and care for my children.

When my husband and I divorced, I was left with a block of land valued at $49,000 and $10,000 cash along with three children to care for. My self-worth had a value of approximately zero. I remember sitting on that block of land, the fear controlling my emotions. **"Who is going to look after me when I'm old?"** These words became a mantra and the fear of being old, alone and penniless triggered a determination inside of me. This fear was a turning point and was my cornerstone towards financial freedom.

Part 2 – Finding the Courage to Change

Sitting on the block with Josh

"Who is going to look after me when I'm old?"

Life after divorce

"Nothing builds self-esteem and self-confidence like accomplishment."

Thomas Carlyle

One of the positive outcomes from my divorce was that I now had control over my own finances. I no longer had to ask any man for permission to spend my money or what I should buy. I loved the fact that for the first time I had to take responsibility for my own actions. I had to sink or swim. Life was now all about making the right choices emotionally and financially. I decided to never again rely on a man for my financial security.

Immediately after my husband left our family, I had to do what most newly divorced women do—pick up the pieces and find a way to move on. My children were devastated at the loss of their father from our family and I was devastated at the loss of the family as a unit. Family had always been an integral part of my life and it was sacrosanct. Regardless of the tumultuous winds that occasionally swept through our family, it remained a family both physically and emotionally and provided a safe harbour against the chaos that sometimes reigned outside.

After our family's separation my thoughts immediately, and out of necessity, turned to money. I applied for a job as a business development manager, and was successful. I found that not only was I a very good cook, I was also a very good sales person and had no trouble exceeding my budget by the end of each month. I put this success down to a certain amount of charm and charisma that I was able to tap into, but mostly to the fact that I tried to communicate with people from my heart. As I didn't have good formal qualifications for my work, I had to rely on my natural instincts and ability to connect with people, and this I was able to do exceptionally well. This success boosted my battered ego and helped improve my self-esteem to the point where I really began to feel a confidence I had not known until this time. The future began to look a little brighter.

Everything has a down side and the down side to this newfound success was that I had to leave my children in day care. I can still see the tears running down my son Matthew's face and him crying, "Mummy, mummy, don't leave me here". As every working mother knows, it is draining to keep the mind on work all day and then take care of children after finishing work in the evening. I felt that I had abandoned my children emotionally even though I knew I loved them above all else. Writing with reference to this time in my life reignites the pain and guilt I felt in trying to provide my children with the quality parenting I believe all children deserve, along with the financial stability I knew we all needed to be able to live a life without deprivation.

I am aware that I was one of but thousands of women trying to negotiate such a hazardous path daily, and that in the years since then the situation single mothers face is little, if any, better. During those years, I was spurred on by the memories of my childhood in Mauritius and the poverty that I saw first-hand every day. The faces belonging to the old people of my childhood never left; their presence swam around in the back of my mind as a constant warning of what might happen should I not be a success. Somewhere in my head the mantra that I was now alone and had only myself to depend on played continually. I grew up believing marriage to be an entitlement and a solid source of security, but for me, it was now gone.

By 1990, I had become so accomplished in my job that I was sourcing many clients for my company from the competition and was subsequently headhunted by a government department and asked to apply for the position of Corporate Accounts Manager at senior management level. Of the 200 applicants, I was given the job. This situation was somewhat unusual, as more often than not a successful applicant for this level would have risen through the ranks of the organisation. This proved to be a source of contention for some employees and negative reactions heightened as time went by. This position came with a very good salary, company car and numerous perks. For me the clincher was that I believed it would enable me to secure a bank loan.

Prior to my divorce, I had bought a block of land at Tanah Merah near Logan, in Queensland. The block of land was on a hill and I would stand on that block and look down over the valley picturing the house that I would build there one day. I pictured where the various rooms would be and what the house would look like on completion. I felt secure in my daydreams; secure in the thought that I could provide a home for my children and in the belief that I would never be one of those poor people that, as a child, I had tried to avoid on the streets of Mauritius.

Standing under the power lines on my block

My family put a lot of pressure on me to rethink my decision and not build on the block. They raised the objections that it was too far from Brisbane and was under a power line. I didn't listen. I wanted to build the home of my vision—a Queenslander with wrap around verandas that would sit high on the hillside, safe in its separation from surrounding houses; a safe place for my children where they could play without me worrying about where they were or who they were with. At this early stage of my career in property, I knew, to some degree, the importance of doing due diligence. However, this purchase was based predominantly on instinct as I think decisions often are during times of heightened stress. I had begun to operate in survival mode during the final stages of the death of my marriage and settling on this property was a significant factor in a quest for survival.

My main motivator in deciding to build on the block at this time was fear and fear can really get you up and running. Fear of being alone, fear of not being able to support myself and my children adequately, fear of being the failure I had been schooled to think I was throughout my childhood. That fear was never very far from the surface and I could literally feel it snapping at my heels every step of the way.

I had the plans drawn up for the house and then went to the bank for a loan. Banks assess their clients based on the three C's:

Capacity – The lender's ability to repay the loan; also known as serviceability
Character – Who the lender is in terms of their employment, business and credit history
Collateral – What security you will be using for the loan

Unfortunately, being female and a single mother were not good boxes to tick on the bank's long list of lending criteria and securing a home loan to turn my dream into reality proved to be a nightmare. The bank refused me a loan even though I met the strict guidelines of the three C's. I had a secure well-paying job, I owned my block of land outright and my character was impeccable in terms of my previous credit history. Unfortunately, my gender and marital status were unappealing.

I was introduced to a broker who had a contact at a different bank; sometimes it's not what you know it's who you know, and my loan was approved. I will be forever grateful to that person for taking the time to see me and having the courage to go against the flow of narrow-minded thinking that typified the banking industry at that time. This first house was the cornerstone of my future wealth and without that being laid, I would have had great difficulty in taking this first step on my path to acquiring a multi-million dollar property portfolio. Although I had to pay this broker a healthy fee, which hurt a bit at the time, in retrospect it was well worth it.

After the loan was approved, I took leave from work and engaged the services of a builder and contracted him to do the job but proceeded as owner builder for the project. I had no idea what to do but I went ahead and did it anyway. I acted on my belief daily; "If you believe you can, you will; if you believe you can't, you won't". In those days, the rules related to building were not as stringent as they are now. I became a builder's apprentice and learnt on the job. I worked with the builder every day, going to the hardware store to pick up materials, frequenting auctions to scour the mishmash of left over building materials, hoping for a find to use in my house. I was new to the business of building; so much of what I bought did not match, and was more often than not a challenge for the builder to fit into the house in a way that satisfied him. I was young and inexperienced in anything to do with building; my obvious vulnerability was not lost on the people I dealt with—especially the men, and many were very patient and went out of their way to help me with things I didn't understand.

During the build, I learnt a lot about building materials and the overall building process. I learnt about tools, how to organise jobs—what needs to be done first and why, how to order materials and why it is important to check what you receive and why you just can't do some things. I learnt the language and how to talk to tradespeople and, most importantly, how not to get on the wrong side of them. This was my apprenticeship and it was to stand me in good stead for later.

I also learnt a lot about financing a build with the most important lesson being that it will usually cost more than you plan for. I purchased all the plumbing items, timber and roofing from personal contacts. All up, the materials and labour cost me $100,000 and the land was worth $50,000. After completion, I was offered $250,000; this meant I had made my first $100,000 in the space of four months!

I cannot begin to describe the feeling of achievement the completion of this house brought to me. I felt I had proved myself to myself and anyone else who had ever doubted my ability to achieve something worthwhile, and I did it on my own without having to lean on a man. I felt invincible.

In reality, this house proved to be the lowest of all my assets in terms of investment performance in the long term, but it provided benefits that were not entirely financial. My children and I loved living there and it is the home of many fond memories. During any difficult time, it comes down to not what you have, but what you do with it. As it turned out, due to my creativity and willingness to have a go, building this house proved to be the basis through which I was able to leverage financing other properties, which would later lead me to financial freedom.

Moving on

"Positive feelings come from being honest about yourself and accepting your personality, and physical characteristics, warts and all; from belonging to a family that accepts you without question."

Willard Scott

After the challenge of building the house had subsided, I began to feel restless again. I now see this as a common theme throughout my life and I am now better prepared for the event, but at the time, it was more of a primal force that propelled me to achieve, without knowing why or how. I was still pining for my ex-husband and waiting for the light bulb to go off in his head that would see him come to his senses and return to his family. It didn't and he didn't, so a little while later I somewhat reluctantly entered into a relationship with a friend I had known for some time. I had three children who missed their father immensely and I wanted to provide a stable family environment for them. In the back of my mind also lurked the thought that, as the mother of three children, no one would want me, and hence the old insecurities began to replay their well-worn tune. The trouble with well-worn tunes is they play the same message over and over again which produce the same emotional results. If you doubt this, try listening to a song from your youth or some significant time in your life—either good or bad—and monitor the feelings that emerge. My cerebral song was that if you are alone you are vulnerable because you may not be able to keep it all together due to your inherent 'lack'. Lack of what—I was never sure, but I felt in the deepest parts inside me that there was a lack of that essential something. This was a lesson from early childhood—from home and from school—and that lesson had put down deep roots. It grew like a creeping vine that takes whatever it can from its food source, strangling growth as it does so.

Two years into the relationship, I found myself pregnant once again but with a partner that was now unemployed and who was not interested in the responsibility of rearing a child and wanted me to terminate the pregnancy. I had a strong premonition that this baby would be a girl and I longed for a daughter. During the pregnancy, I suffered some prejudice at work due to being an unwed mother and I found it increasingly difficult to drag myself out of bed and off to work each morning. Apparently, an unwed pregnant woman was not ideal to hold the position I had and I was subsequently demoted to a lower position, although retaining the same salary. To be fair, it wasn't only my work colleagues that disapproved of my pregnancy; I don't think my mother was too impressed about her daughter now becoming an unwed mother. I have no doubt that she thought she had successfully guided me safely through the young rebellious years and now here I was, mother of three children and her worst nightmare saw the light of day. I was still greatly influenced by my mother, as our relationship from childhood was deep. I felt bad for her, as I knew as a staunch Catholic how embarrassed she would be. This increased my anxiety level considerably which affected me and I worried that it would affect my unborn child. As usual, this turmoil brewed well below the surface but erupted at various unpredictable times and usually with much volatility.

I woke up one morning knowing that I could not continue to work under such conditions, so I resigned. It was an instinctive rather than a rational decision, coming from that primal part of the brain that underpins survival. I didn't think about details like how I would take care of my children, I just decided that enough was enough and once again, I believed in my own ability to survive. I decided to go onto the single parent's pension. For me, this was a brave decision but it was one that I felt was right at the time as I had my physical and mental health to deal with and neither were great. While the decision to quit work felt right, regularly fronting up to Centrelink to fill in my form didn't. The fall from manager to unemployment benefit recipient was not an easy transition—even when brought about by my own free will. With the old negative stuff playing in my head, it didn't take long for my self-esteem to plummet to an all-time low. It happened automatically as it had done previously. My inner self knew the route and navigated it with little opposition.

My daughter Jessica was born and she truly was a bright star in a rather dim sky. After her birth, I suffered post-natal depression; I was no doubt a victim waiting to be claimed by this terrible condition. Did you know that one in seven women suffer from post-natal depression? My life situation no doubt played a role in the unfolding of this sad story. Alone, not married and with a fourth child I had few resources to call upon. I had no knowledge of this disorder and was not about to admit to anything that I thought may resemble some sort of mental illness, so I struggled on day after day trying to do what I could not possibly do. Pride did not allow me to acknowledge my feelings of not being able to cope or ask for help. People who knew me suggested I seek medical help and take anti-depressants, but I refused to listen or follow any advice. I was in denial that anything was wrong with me while all the time feeling totally debilitated and out of control. I slept most of the time and found it almost impossible to get out of bed and attend to normal household chores.

My daughter, Jessica

My son Benjamin was fourteen years old at the time and often assumed the role of father to Jessica. He fed her and changed her nappies. He showed maturity well beyond his years during that trying time. Eventually my sister took my two youngest children for six months to allow me time to recuperate. I remain ever grateful for her many acts of kindness to my children and I over the years, and the positive affect she has had on our lives. My mother was a constant in our lives and she proved to be a pillar of support on many occasions when all was not right in my world.

One thing I am truly grateful for is that my children never lacked a sense of belonging. Although there were periods of instability, they always felt a secure attachment.

From creativity to chaos—and back again

"Every form of addiction is bad, no matter whether the narcotic be alcohol or morphine or idealism."

Carl Jung

At this point, life for me resembled an attempt to cross a river by jumping precariously from one slippery stepping-stone to the next. I would wake up each morning hoping to make the next step but not knowing if or for how long I would be able to keep my balance and if I couldn't, how and where I would fall. I made many valiant, but mostly vain, attempts to redefine my life. I read book after book about self-development but the more I tried to put the advice into practice the more I perceived myself as being a failure. I constantly felt guilty for not being able to be both mother and father for my children. I may have been there for them physically but I was absent emotionally. I desperately wanted a father for Jessica and a stable, normal family life for us all. While my sons experienced some fragments of what had once been family life, in that their father regularly met with them, my daughter had only me.

Depression is a non-discriminatory illness. It attacks all intellectual and socio-economic levels equally as well as both genders and all ethnic groups. No part of my life escaped this plague. The 'black dog' left his paw marks everywhere and my intimate life was a prime target. The events of my childhood had set the stage for me to be a loner, but not just the everyday garden variety; I was a co-dependent loner. I was really bad at establishing and keeping healthy relationships and therefore I worked better alone—less complicated. However, due to my deep-seated insecurity I needed someone upon whom I could lean when the going got tough. And the going always gets tough at some point. Being in a relationship also meant there was someone there for me to try to keep in control and thereby bolster my lagging self-esteem and try, by proxy, to create some order in my own life. Unfortunately, as relationships were never a thing at which I excelled, whenever things did hum along smoothly and I began to feel happy, I inevitably sabotaged them to get myself back to my comfort zone—misery. Misery was my safety blanket. Misery was what I knew and where I felt comfortable. I defined myself through it and I was addicted to it.

During this period of my life, there was a national downturn in property investing for many people and I did not have a lot on my mind in terms of buying, selling and developing. It was during this lull in my work that I met a man with who I fell madly in love. He was my agony and my ecstasy. We were together on and off for the next fifteen years—more off than on. We had trouble staying together for more than two weeks at a stretch but couldn't stay apart either. It was tumultuous to say the least but I was addicted to it. When I first met him, I thought he was wise beyond what I knew. He taught me a lot about business and how to communicate with people in a business situation and I owe much of my later success in business to his tutelage. He reinforced a belief in me that I could do anything I wanted to do. I found our ability to communicate exhilarating compared to my previous relationships and sometimes we would talk so much my children would tell us to be quiet. He became a father figure to my children and contributed to their lives in a positive way.

However, addiction is addiction and regardless of its form, the results are much the same. When we had an argument and separated, I would have panic attacks that were so severe I would pace up and down the hallway, too scared to close my eyes and sleep for fear I would die and my children would be left alone. When I did sleep, I would wake up in a panic, feeling that I was choking and about to die. I would have to go out in the middle of the night to buy lozenges to clear my throat. Having lozenges became essential for survival during those dark days and nights of isolation. They were my life support. My life was ruled alternatively by ecstasy and fear. Being in an addictive relationship is much the same as being addicted to a substance, when the supply is not available; the body reacts in a number of different ways: depression, mood swings, feelings of helplessness and physical illness.

I hung onto the relationship with that man as though my life depended upon it. The dependency immobilised my life to the point where normal everyday functions became impossible. I was unable to have a shower for fear the water would stop me breathing.

Sometimes this meant that I would not shower for days and just sit around the house in my dressing gown. When my daughter arrived home from school I would be sitting in the same place as when she left in the morning. Eating became an emotional crutch and I gained a significant amount of weight. I was reliving the life of my mother but the fog was too dense for me to recognise the similarity. I had lived with internal chaos from the age of five when I used to run home from school to save my mother and the chaos and pain had become part of the fabric of who I had become. I began to accept depression as part of my life. It became a familiar occurrence that repeated itself in horrifyingly familiar cycles. The instability and insecurity my children suffered during that time must have been horrific. I wish I had the skills to make better life choices during that time and I wish I had the means of erasing the residual pain from their heart.

My dysfunctional behaviours came in a variety of forms—some with positive aspects and some without. Fortunately, I was never attracted to alcohol or drugs so not having to deal with substance abuse problems has always been a huge plus. I got my highs from taking risks in my business ventures and this always supplied the adrenalin that made me feel alive. As I inherited my father's workaholic nature, adrenalin was not usually in short supply. After an episode of depression and inactivity, I would reactivate myself, and my passion for property would resurface.

I now see life as being the embodiment of opposites: darkness and light, success and failure, chaos and calmness, confidence and fear, wealth and poverty. I know all about opposites because opposites ran my life. Just when I thought I had captured the calm, chaos would appear and I would lurch towards it with a familiarity that defied logical thought. When I thought I had love, betrayal snaked its way into the relationship. Success was always dogged by failure and confidence gave way to fear—without fail. I know that to discuss the relationship between opposites can be slippery, depending on one's philosophical or scientific view, but for me, opposites are simple; they are tangible and they are the fabric of my earliest memories.

To me, my mother personifies this concept. While nurturing in many ways—a wonderful cook, devout in her religious convictions and open minded for her generation in terms of her interest in self-development and spiritual growth—she evidenced contrasting behaviours that created chaos and insecurity within the family. I now understand that my mother suffered from depression, but as a young child, I only knew that my mother was a constant source of fear and insecurity although during my childhood I depended upon her completely. It was only in later years that I could identify the feelings and give them a name. In my mother, I began to see a reflection of myself and it frightened me.

From pain to pleasure—eventually

"We cannot change anything if we cannot change our thinking."

Santosh Kalwar

Although I hated pain and pursued pleasure voraciously, pain was my constant companion. Pain was what I knew and pain was what I trusted. Pain never let me down. Pain was always there. It was my truth. We were uneasy soul mates and in order to avoid the negativity, I would become active, super active. Working provided the adrenalin I needed to feel alive and the feeling of being alive again was intoxicating. The activity of work kept my mind occupied and out of dangerous territory. I would temporarily forget my anxiety, anguish and misery. After bouts of depression, I would work like crazy renovating houses and looking for possible property deals. I would go to bed each night satisfied that I had worked hard and usually accomplished a great deal, but somewhere inside my head was still the question: "What is this all for? Is there a reason for my being here?"

Three years had passed and I was still receiving the single parent's pension and finding it increasingly difficult to make ends meet. My children went to a private Catholic school and meeting this and other financial commitments became increasingly difficult, to the point that I was teetering on the edge of bankruptcy. I had debt collectors knocking on my door and

Part 2 – From Pain to Pleasure—Eventually

more than once I sent one of the children to the door to say, "Mummy isn't home". It is fair to say that at this point I was feeling pretty disillusioned. Not a lot was going right in my life and the future was looking very bleak. It was when things were at their absolute worst that an angel appeared and provided me with an opportunity to make things right in my world. This particular angel was my sister; a woman who has spent a large part of her life helping others less fortunate through her deeds and words and when I needed the help most, she was there. My sister, Marie-France, and my brother-in-law mortgaged their property to help me out financially.

I believe that at significant times people will enter into our lives for a reason; to teach a lesson which may be transmitted in a positive way, or may in fact, cause pain. Whichever form the lesson takes it is an opportunity for us to grow and become wiser, learning to trust our own intuition and realise that everything operates according to a plan. With the financial help from my sister, I was able to get back on my feet and eventually I pulled myself out of my depression. I feel the best way to pull out of a depression is to find something that you can really pour your heart into. I decided it was time to get creative once again. I came to realise that I became depressed when I thought about all the mistakes I had made in my life. I am a firm believer in "What you think, you become", so following this philosophy had been able to become successful in my business life but my relationships had been a miserable failure. This positive period signalled a new phase in my life.

Although my journey had been a hard and painful one, mainly due to the poor choices I had made, I began to turn my life around from misery to mastery and develop the confidence I had yearned for so long. How did I do it? I set a goal and I made a plan as to how I was going to get there. I made a concerted effort to change my mindset and tried to bring more discipline into all aspects of my life. I read book after book on financial literacy, emotional growth and how to effectively overcome challenges in life. I read whatever I thought would educate me to become a better, more stable breadwinner and mother. The goal I made for myself was to become a millionaire and I set about achieving it. To do so I was prepared to make short-term sacrifice for long-term gain.

I was very short on funds and still needed to create cash flow. When cash was what I needed there was virtually no limit to my creativity, some of which seemed more than crazy to my friends and acquaintances —and occasionally to myself. I used to attend auctions and buy a random selection of items; if I thought I could sell it for a profit—I bought it. One auction saw me come away with three-hundred pairs of Italian shoes. How do you dispose of three-hundred pairs of Italian shoes? You sell on a party plan. I had weekend shoe parties for weeks, eventually selling all the shoes and making a tidy profit. On another occasion, I bought ten mattresses and sold them through advertisements in the paper. Whatever I had was always for sale if there was a profit to be made. One morning I woke my kids up early and hurried them out of bed as there was a buyer at the door for their beds. It's not difficult to see why people thought I was crazy—and maybe I was, but this was about survival and I was prepared to do whatever I needed to do to survive, and prosper. And it wasn't all bad. When you get the hang of thinking outside of the box, anything is possible. The 'entrepreneurial instinct' kicks in and it's all go. Money and adrenalin can be powerful motivators and with each success, the stakes become higher. My new mantra was "Thrive and Survive", and I did.

A good part of the 1990s were not particularly happy years for real estate investors although people with more experience than me did continue to make money. The days of seventeen percent interest rates put quite a dampener on real estate investment and during these years, I didn't pursue real estate investment as a way of growing wealth. However, from experience I did know that this too would pass and investing in real estate would once again be a possibility for me. These years became what I affectionately refer to as 'my investment hibernation years'.

During these years I made a huge effort to address the personal issues I now realised I had. It was often one step forward and several steps back, exacerbated by my very volatile relationship. However, it was also a time of growing consciousness through which I continued to develop, albeit slowly at times. I realised I had to make an investment in myself if I ever hoped to be able to invest in the business enterprises I envisaged.

I realised that to "Thrive and Survive" I needed to develop multiple streams of income and the linchpin to this was myself, and my ability to function in a proactively sustainable way. I kept close to my heart the words of Jim Rohn, **"Learn to work harder on yourself than you do on your job. If you work at your job you'll make a living; if you work on yourself you'll make a fortune".** I did begin to work on myself, and eventually I did make a fortune.

I have read many books throughout my life and have come to believe that when you need the teacher one will appear—and that is often in the form of a book. Many of the greatest gifts I have received in my life were books. I come from a family of readers and spiritual books always had a place in our home. My sister, Marie, would always give me a book or a card with words of wisdom as a gift for Christmas or birthdays. I sometimes thought, "Why does she always lecture me?" but now I see those as my most treasured gifts. Life without books is like a body without a soul. Books can take the place of a mentor, a trainer, a friend or a companion. They instruct, motivate, nurture, enlighten, encourage, provoke and take you to new places and provide new experiences. During my many house moves, I have left behind furniture and other belongings, but never my library. Books give unconditional love—they are always there when you need them most. My books are like my children.

At one point in the mid-nineties and during one of my most vulnerable periods, a woman who I barely knew gave me a book entitled 'Unlimited Power' by

Anthony Robbins. I read the book and consciously worked very hard to put the advice into action every day of my life. I began what was for me, the mother of all learning curves. I learnt about love. I learnt about fear and I learnt about who I could be. I learnt to 'face my fears and do it anyway'. I learnt the importance of being me. I would wake up every morning and tell myself how great I was and that I could do anything I chose; be anything I wanted to be if I had the desire, the discipline and the determination to reach my destination.

While there were areas of my life within which I could definitely feel improvement, moving from debilitating depression to emotional stability is a big task and a big ask—it isn't a smooth transition. I continued to experience the now very familiar cycles of functionality with debility. I pushed myself very hard in dealing with my psychological demons while at the same time working towards my goals of financial success. I was a mother, a businesswoman and a renovator. Life was all go.

Using property to move ahead

"Anyone who has never made a mistake has never tried anything new."

Albert Einstein

While I had been putting a lot of effort into my personal development, I sorely needed to do something to get myself back on track financially. I studied and became a finance broker and went from earning $300 per week on a single parent's pension to $1,500 per week as a broker. It seemed a natural 'life progression' for me to go down this path. I established my own consultancy and I enjoyed being able to help people achieve their goals that involved needing financial help and advice. I felt a sense of achievement by doing something that I found rewarding both intellectually and emotionally and at the same time assisting other people—often women in a similar life situation to my own.

There had been a lull of three years since my last property deal but I sensed now was the right time to get back to working with property. After scouring property advertisements with the specific goal of finding a property to which I could add value and on sell for a profit, I eventually found a house in Moorooka, a suburb about six kilometres from the centre of Brisbane. The house was on a 1,000 square metre block, giving me enough room to split, build and profit. I paid $90,000 for the property and extracted $10,000 from my line of credit as a deposit. I was totally green. I knew nothing about subdividing property and I had no one to help me through the process. It really was a case of 'fake it till you make it.' Looking back, it probably was just as well I had little idea of the abundant technicalities and pitfalls that come with dealing with council in order to get approval for subdivision. I seemed to spend my life talking, writing, calculating and waiting in line. To make this vision a reality I purchased an old Queenslander from Coorparoo and moved it to the rear of the property, thereby giving me two properties instead of one.

The subdivision at Moorooka

This time I decided to engage the services of a builder to do the whole project. This decision proved to be yet another sharp learning curve as I failed to check his credentials and he in turn, failed to deliver—in a big way. From this experience, I learnt the importance of always asking to see an ABN, Gold Card and qualifications to complete the job successfully. I also learnt that it is necessary to get more than one quote and not to disregard the informed opinion of other people who have had similar experiences and learnt the lessons contained therein. Unfortunately, I have not always listened to other people when it would have been prudent to do so. While I have learnt that one cannot continually be swayed by the negativity of others, there are also times when to listen and learn is the best way to achieve a goal. I can definitely say, "I did it my way", but in this instance, my way was the hard way. I was long on determination but somewhat short on humility. I made many mistakes during this learning process that could have been avoided, but probably the most important thing I learnt was the importance of having a sound workable system in place. This saves on time, money and angst.

The problems really started when I realised the house was too large to manoeuvre to the rear of the property and had to be cut in half. This increased the cost and time needed to complete the project considerably. Needless to say, I have never repeated this mistake. One thing it is not possible to control is the weather and this too conspired against me. It rained non-stop for two weeks while the house had no roof, which resulted in a significant amount of extra work both inside and outside.

Never one to waste resources, I had my children on site helping out. They sometimes complained about the inequality of it all; they were there working all weekend while their friends were off doing kid stuff. While this may seem a bit harsh, it did prove to be the training ground for my son Benjamin, who moved to Singapore to work as a Project Manager for Marina Sands Casino where he was involved in its construction.

Learning to fly

An eagle's egg somehow found its way into a turkey's nest. The unsuspecting mother turkey did her duty and sat on all the eggs until they hatched, then raised them all together as good little turkey chicks. As often happens, mother had some issues with the one that was a bit different, but with turkeys not being too bright mother didn't click that the 'difficult' chick wasn't a turkey at all. She did her best to teach the odd chick how to behave like a good turkey and not cause trouble. She taught it to scratch and peck for food and scurry along the ground with all the other chicks. Just like any good mum, she cautioned it about the dangers of flying and told the chick how it was much safer to stay close to the ground and not to draw attention to itself by trying to be different. She worried about its weird appetite and stressed about the fact that it was always hungry and trying to steal food from the others. Secretly, mother turkey thought this little one was not only a bit odd but quite ugly, and wondered where these anomalies could have come from. Like all mothers, she probably blamed the dad—or at least his family.

Meanwhile, the odd turkey chick was growing up with huge issues of its own. Somehow, it felt different but didn't quite know why. It began to get a complex about looking different from the other chicks, and their constant scratching and pecking in the dirt at everything got on its nerves. They spent so much time looking for food yet barely seemed to scratch out a living with the worms, bugs and whatever else it was they ate. Hunger was another problem. Odd chick always felt hungry. It knew for sure it was hungry for food but, there always seemed to be something else it hungered for but the chick could never quite figure out exactly what it was that was missing. As odd chick grew older things just got worse. There was the problem with the wings. Odd chick's wings were huge to the point of being a real hindrance to others when they were fully spread. It tried its best to flap like a turkey but the more it tried the more hopeless it all seemed to be and the more despondent odd chick became, until eventually it had very little self-esteem at all. Mother turkey virtually gave up on it and accepted the fact that there is one in every family, and decided to just focus on the normal chicks. Things just went from bad to worse for odd chick and it really felt like it was going to die. It was in a very bad place.

Then one day, all of a sudden, something happened—as it often does when one has hit rock bottom. Odd chick looked upwards; it had never really looked upwards before because turkeys don't really do that, they keep focused on the ground right in front of them. But when odd chick looked up it saw other creatures up in the sky flying around, unafraid. This was a bit confronting because turkey mother had always warned against trying to fly. But there they were—flying, and looking really happy about it. Without really thinking odd chick spread its wings and then fate seemed to take over; a voice from the space above called and odd chick answered. It flapped it wings and with minimum fuss had lifted off. Odd chick flew higher and higher, soaring over the land it had only known from ground level. Everything looked very different from the sky; the trees and rocks that always seemed so big were now very small. Its flying companions were different from the turkeys too; they looked just like odd chick. It took a little while but eventually odd chick started to feel quite comfortable up there near the clouds. It started to feel like home. Odd chick no longer felt odd; in fact, odd chick found it had a lot in common with this new group of eagles. Odd chick finally figured it out; odd chick was an eagle and not odd at all—in fact it was quite normal.

Based on a story by Garret John LoPorto

I can identify with this story. For a long time I thought I was a turkey and I suffered all the problems associated with trying to fit in. When I was young, I was upset at being different, of not being smart. I was afraid to look up in case I saw something I couldn't deal with so I kept my focus firmly on the ground in front of me. I knew there was another way; I knew I could fly if I had the chance but I was afraid of taking the chance so I just tried harder to focus and fit in. I scratched in the ground for worms but deep inside me I wanted to try and find another food source. It took me until I was in my forties to truly believe I could fly. Once I understood why I was different and that it was okay to be different, things started to fall into place. I made an effort to heal the wounds that had been oozing for so long and chase the dreams I had, until now, only dreamed.

The eagle flies south

"He who would learn to fly one day must first learn to stand and walk and run and climb and dance; one cannot fly into flying."

Friedrich Nietzsche

In 1999, a girlfriend of mine basically forced me to attend a Lebanese ball held in Sydney. I didn't really want to go as I knew everyone would be speaking Lebanese and I wouldn't be able to socialise at all. I reluctantly agreed to attend just to please her but I was prepared for a boring night. I found myself seated next to a man who seemed happy to chat and he eventually asked me what I did for a living. I told him I was a finance broker. He must have liked what he saw as he asked me to come to his office the next day and meet his boss as the company wanted to employ a finance broker to head their new office in Clarence Street, Sydney. I was somewhat surprised by this offer but decided as I had nothing to lose I'd go along anyway. I managed to bluff my way through the interview with the skills I had honed over the preceding years, what I termed my "Acting as if…" strategy. Apparently, I had managed to refine this skill to an acceptable degree as I was offered the position. They asked me what it would take for me to move to Sydney and I jokingly replied, "A new BMW or Mercedes convertible". The next day I received a call offering me the position of general manager—with the BMW. To say I was surprised would be an understatement and I'm not sure whether it was ego or bravado that prompted me to accept without much thought as to the consequences.

Looking back, I see that little girl who had always been teased about being slow at school, who as a young adult felt inferior to her ex-husband and his contemporaries and who as a mother struggled to provide for her children and make a future for them, being offered a position that she would never have thought could possibly come her way. I can see why I grabbed it with both hands; I saw it as a door to freedom. Life experience had somehow taught me to consider myself inferior to my contemporaries, which was not always a bad thing as this also nurtured in me the homespun philosophy of "Let freedom be the guide rather than fear". I'm not sure this always works but at the time, it was the light by which my steps were guided and I made the leap of faith.

I rented out my Brisbane properties and moved to Rose Bay in Sydney. It was a homecoming for me but a big adjustment for my children. I had arrived home from my meeting with my soon-to-be boss and said, "Right kids, let's start packing we are moving to Sydney". No doubt if I had given more thought to the move it would not have happened, but being on adrenalin high with the smell of success wafting up my nostrils and the BMW well within my sights, there was no time nor reason to think too deeply. I may have got off to a shaky start in life but now, I had all the confidence I would need to succeed, and confidence is power. I took with me the skills I had and the rest I learnt on the job.

My colleagues in Sydney were very different from my former colleagues in Brisbane. I became friends with people who had authored their own success and their mindset helped me change mine. I have come to know a very successful lawyer and an accountant who gave me free advice that helped me appreciate the importance of content knowledge and the necessity of creating a team of experts in order to limit risk and increase the chance of success.

One man I was introduced to was a very well known property developer who was the catalyst for taking property to the next level. He introduced me to his clients and I was able to finance many of the deals for him. I saw him transform an old bread factory in Paddington into upmarket apartments, and while I was fascinated by what he did, I never thought I would be able to achieve anything similar. In the deep recesses of my mind, I thought such success was confined to the male domain, but I watched what he did very carefully and continually challenged my own thinking as to what I could possibly do in the future to make a bigger difference in my life. That question constantly played round the edges of my mind. The answers varied slightly depending on the situation I was working in at the time, but the question was always constant. I was in constant contact with very wealthy people and I also wanted to become wealthy, but I was also very conscious that time was running out for me to be able to make this leap into financial freedom.

Life was all go and I went as much as possible. I tried never to miss an opportunity to learn, to better myself and to hone my skills. Every day was an adventure filled with learning new things, with the excitement of meeting new people and hearing their stories and experiences. Then, disaster struck—with the swiftness and brutality, that always accompanies disaster. The Japanese company I worked for went bankrupt. My job was gone, my salary was gone and the BMW was gone. The Rose Bay apartment rent was huge and the children's school fees were high. So what did I do? I did what I knew best—I went into a depression. I had spent a lot of time and energy since my last lapse into depression in an effort to 'depression proof' myself against future episodes, but I was still vulnerable as circumstances were about to prove.

My employment situation was compounded by my guilt in having upended my children's lives, taking them out of school and moving them to Sydney, only to fail. I once again hibernated in the bedroom and spent a lot of time sleeping. I neglected my home, my children and myself. I was incapacitated by this unexpected downturn in my life both emotionally and financially. To compound my feelings of worthlessness I again applied for a single parent's pension in order to survive. My brain functioned so poorly this was the only solution I could think of. As the black clouds gathered in my head, my thoughts focused once again on survival, survival for my children and myself. My anxiety heightened to a level that I could not see the future and

I spent each day re-running 'worst case scenarios' in my head as though they were reality.

My children missed school to the extent that a teacher who lived downstairs came up to see me one day and asked if I needed any help. He had noticed that I never put the bin out and assumed not all must be well upstairs. He very kindly offered to drive my children to school. During our conversation, he asked me what type of work I did and when I told him I was a finance broker, he replied that he was looking to refinance his property. I told him that I may have a problem in putting out the bin but I would have no problem in refinancing his property. I asked him to give me a couple of days to clear my desk and then come back and I would sort out his property matters. Immediately, I decided to stop feeling sorry for myself, and get back to work. Little did I know that this misfortune would be the springboard for later opportunity that would indeed see me flourish financially; providing the answers and opportunities for those questions that had constantly whirled around in my head while working in my recently relinquished job.

The roaring forties

"I feel that the greatest opportunity for doing is the opportunity to do more."

Dr Jonas Salk

The forties (and fifties) generally have a bit of a bad reputation. They are often approached with trepidation and negative thoughts of midlife crises, divorce, singleness and the associated horrors of midlife online dating, not to mention financial ruin—or near ruin. Whether men or women suffer more through this rocky midlife rite of passage depends on whom you talk to. Statistically, women have it over the men in terms of financial difficulty. They usually get to keep the kids while the departed dad gets to live the single life once again. Women's income is more likely to take a dive and at this time of life, they may be more likely to be needed by ailing parents as a primary or secondary caregiver. Around this time the kids are somewhere in the teenage years and finding their stride in terms of creating havoc, be it behavioural, financial or both. Having to upgrade to keep a job, particularly in a male dominated field, can be the proverbial 'icing on the cake' when a myriad of other life issues are clamouring for attention. While my 'forties' were a mixed bag and I got to sample most of the above, those years did eventually see me achieve many of my goals and savour the taste of success.

The first lesson I learnt from my experience with the company in Sydney was that it is not smart to rely on one source of income. Times had changed and somehow I had missed the shift. We tend to learn from our parents and even though we chart our own course as we grow, certain things tend to stick. With me, and possibly others of my generation, training for and having one major skill and source of income was generally normal. I know other people may have clicked onto the momentous change that was rocking many workplaces and people's lives, but I was a bit slow. Much of my early experience still shaped my thinking and to this point, I was still looking for that one magic bullet that was to make me happy and wealthy. While working in the company I thought I had found it; now I realised I had not. So, what to do? My first step into the arena of the multi-skilled was to get my real estate licence. Having dabbled in investing, renovating, brokering and now selling, I set my sights on developing. Selling property to clients in Sydney allowed me to develop a feel for the property market from a different perspective than formerly, and I had a very strong feeling that the market in Brisbane was about to take off. My selling career had been successful and my earnings had been in the six-figure bracket for some time so I was in the position to make the move back to Brisbane when my intuition told me the time was right. I now had some money to invest in property development and I was eager to make a start.

Old salts of the property market say that the property tide ebbs and flows in seven-year cycles, so using that as an indicator it seemed to me the time was ripe for positive change. We moved back to Brisbane.

My focus had now changed somewhat from the major concern of how I was going to provide for my children, to how I was going to provide for myself in retirement. Given my reasonably well established life in Sydney and adequate income, to move again was a risk but I felt then as I do now, if a risk is not taken in order to avoid possible failure, the possibility of success is sacrificed. The person who risks nothing—does nothing. Sometimes the risk proves costly but I feel to avoid risk is the greater hazard as we never understand or achieve our full potential. As I made the move from Sydney, I now had in my arsenal: my experience as a finance broker, a real estate agent, an owner builder, a renovator and now my goal was to become a property developer. I felt ready to move to the next level.

Back in Brisbane, I found a block of four units in Paddington, which I thought were a good buy and presented a good opportunity for future growth. I prepared my documents and went off to see the bank—déjà vu. The banks didn't share my enthusiasm for the property and thought it a poor risk. I tried three different banks but was declined by each as many banks do not accept unit blocks as security. Finally, a broker suggested I try a specific bank, which at the time was giving ninety percent loans. I did, and the loan was approved. With the ninety percent loan approval, all I needed was $10,000. I refinanced my Tanah Merah house into a line of credit to finance the units. The units proved to be an excellent kick-off point for my investment journey although, had I not understood the intricacies of banking I would not have had the knowledge or the courage to go ahead with the purchase.

Block of units at Paddington

I purchased the units at a reasonable price for a very good reason—they were in terrible condition. Each unit was occupied by less than optimal tenants and were covered with vines that claimed part of the internal as well as external walls, but they were each returning $150.00 per week. The building also needed underpinning which was off-putting to other buyers but I decided it was worth the risk. I am a bit of a scrooge by nature so when confronted with the task of renovating these units I rolled up my sleeves and started to do the work myself rather than employ tradespeople. This was another in a long line of lessons that needed to be learnt. Having been a single mother and having spent some time as the recipient of a single parent's pension, I had developed a 'poverty' mentality that, to this day, lurks in the recesses of my mind.

I haggled my way through the renovation and when I did pay someone to do a job I wasted time and energy trying to save money. This wasted a lot of time and was the cause of much heartache. However, within three months the value of the property increased considerably.

I then refinanced the units to buy a townhouse in Toowong and a house in Bardon. I also bought other properties during this period at Salisbury, Taringa, Toowong and Baulkham Hills in Sydney. I bought these properties with a specific goal in mind, to buy and on sell for a profit in order to accumulate funds for other investment properties.

Renovation at Bardon

From residential to commercial

"Life is inherently risky. There is only one big risk you should avoid at all costs, and that is the risk of doing nothing."

Denis Waitley

Property Investor Magazine article

2004 was the year of my financial breakthrough and this is when I really started to make money with property. I was featured in Property Investor Magazine and I had become a self-made millionaire in less than three years.

I sold the house that I retained from the subdivision in Moorooka to finance the purchase of the commercial property in Milton. From information gleaned from other property investors, I had come to believe that commercial property was risky so I was rather hesitant about the purchase. The commercial property in Milton was put into a family trust rather than being in my name as the other properties had been up until that point in time.

My first commercial property at Milton

When I first saw this building, I felt there was a reason I needed to buy it. In the back of my mind there was a sense that this building would play an important role in my life in some way and the gem of an idea that took root then has never died and is about to flourish.

The next acquisition to my growing property family was a mall in Moorooka. I clearly remember walking through the mall one day in 1992 and having a premonition that I would own it. I guess the mall was meant to be. By this time, I had acquired a business partner who was a lawyer.

My business partner called me early one morning to tell me that the mall was for sale. At the time, properties in Brisbane were selling fast so I rushed over to the site and made a quick decision to buy. I found who the agent was and made an appointment to meet with him. I wanted the property but knew there were other buyers circling the prey, so I told the agent that if he would organise for a contract to be signed immediately I would give him management rights to the building. I signed the contract. When a buyer finds what they believe to be a good deal it is imperative that the contract is signed as quickly as possible, and then do the due diligence. If it proves to be unsatisfactory, the offer can always be withdrawn. This is particularly true in a hot market. I refinanced the commercial property in Milton to buy the mall in Moorooka.

Once again, the mall was dilapidated and all the shops were empty. I did a cosmetic renovation and rented out the shops. Not only is this property returning a good yield, but it is a development site with the potential for high-rise development. Having a business partner made this purchase more viable as we did this as a joint venture. As he is also my lawyer, I benefit from his advice and expertise in a variety of ways. Collaboration enables me to expand and diversify my investments, providing a positive and prosperous outcome. As mentioned earlier, being prepared to take a calculated risk is essential if you wish to move forward. Without having taken the risk of moving to Sydney, I would never have had the confidence to go ahead with the commercial property deals. All my previous deals were part of the training; building up my 'property muscles' and enabling me to engage heavier weights.

The mall in Moorooka

Looking out over the back yard of the Paddington units one day, I told my children that at some time in the future I would buy the adjoining rear block. To do so would mean I would own quite a nice parcel of land in Paddington. I bought it in 2006 and it was my only property that was negatively geared.

Working with property is basically being able to do two things well: have a feel for property and know whether it has potential and being able to crunch the numbers to see if the potential can be turned into a possibility. I love the numbers and have often just stood on a piece of land or in a property and juggled them around in my head to see if they stack up. I inherited this from my father and I am thankful to him for passing this ability on to me.

Winds of change

"Belief in oneself is one of the most important bricks in building any successful venture."

Lydia M Child

By 2007, I felt my confidence had returned—perhaps a little too much, and I decided to go for broke.

It was shaping up to be a great year and I was full of confidence and clarity about what I wanted to do and where I wanted to go. I made the right choice in buying development sites that were situated close to water and with views. My communication skills were well oiled after my work in Sydney, so I was able to negotiate the deals in ways that best suited my overall purpose. I let my creativity take over as I designed buildings for the sites and collaborated with other investors to increase cash flow. All was good in Orane's world.

I bought a 1.5-acre block of land at Caboolture on which I planned to build a block of fifty-one units. It was a beautiful flat block overlooking the river and as I stood there, I could literally see the building as it would stand—with my name on it! The words of van Gogh frequently rang in my head, ***"I dream my painting then I paint my dream".*** I did lots of dreaming about that building.

I dream my painting then I paint my dream

I then bought another property at Newport. My intention was to stay there for a year, renovate it and sell for a profit. The house stood on a canal and had its own jetty. It was what I term a 'lifestyle house', not one that would really increase significantly in value even in a robust financial market. With this house, I made a fatal mistake, which goes to show that even though I had quite a lot of experience in property investing, I still had lessons to learn. This house was my first 'emotional' buy. In buying this house, I let emotion be the basis for a financial decision and in doing so broke one of the basic rules of investing. I was soon to pay for that mistake.

I also purchased another block of units facing the beach, fulfilling another dream of mine—to have a beachfront property. My business partner put his house up as leverage and we set about getting approval for twelve luxury units.

As I was on a roll, I bought another property not too long after the previous purchases, a three-bedroom townhouse across from Suttons Beach at Margate on the Redcliffe Peninsula. The townhouse was new when I purchased it from a friend who developed the property. When buying this property I made yet another inexcusable mistake; I didn't get a building inspection. For this mistake I also paid a high price. The property had defects that created ongoing problems with water and all-in-all has been a bit of a nightmare.

As I view investing as a business (apart from my one digression), I view my properties as assets and liabilities that have to perform financially in terms of the yield they produce. My investments are financed by the bank and paid for by my tenants. As I am an investor and not a speculator, I understand that the real estate market goes through different cycles so the strategy I use depends on the nature of the market at the time. Although I have witnessed variations in the property cycle and seen specific areas or types of property affected by certain conditions, I did not see the Global Financial Crisis coming. I had overcapitalised and while this may have worked to my favour in a strong market, it did not serve me well when the GFC hit. I had been too optimistic rather than planning for 'worst case scenario'.

They say that if you look at the seven people you associate with most in your life—there lies your future. For me, this proved to be a truism as my friends were my business partner who is a lawyer, my then partner who was an accountant and other friends who were bank managers. I had the right associates to help me get out of trouble.

The GFC taught me many valuable lessons about how to handle property more efficiently in terms of finances. As finances continued to tighten due to the effects of the GFC, the banks did an about turn and rather than wooing their customers with loan approvals, they began to call in their loans. I did not know that this was possible so I was caught unawares when this started to happen. Due to the fact that one of my loans was a business loan for my commercial property and cross collateralised with my residential property made my situation all the more vulnerable. All my loans were with one bank; a mistake I will never make again. Within one foul swoop, I went from being 'valued customer' to 'high risk'.

As the financial tsunami gathered force, I frantically began refinancing my loans. This unforseen event cost me thousands of dollars as in some cases I had borrowed one-hundred percent of the loan and I could now only refinance at eighty percent, effectively costing me $200,000 for every one-million dollars of debt. This situation meant that I had to put the developments that I had been about to begin on hold.

Re-enter the shadow

"You have power over your mind—not outside events. Realise this, and you will find strength."

Marcus Aurelius

Meanwhile in dealing with the ever-increasing challenges thrown up by the GFC, I returned yet again to my comfort zone. I became depressed and felt that I had no control over what was happening in my life. My mind dredged up those early lessons in helplessness that I had learnt so well as a child and laid them out for me to sample once again. At this stage in my life, I had entered menopause. By now, my older children had left home and my teenage daughter had carved out a rebellious niche not uncommon to teenage years and was, basically, giving me hell. She became rebellious and her choices of friends were less than desirable. She started taking drugs and abusing alcohol. I would often be woken in the middle of the night with phone calls from the hospital. She was trying to come to terms with the fact that of my four children she was the one who did not have contact with her father. This of course sent my guilt barometer through the roof, creating an equally downward spiral in my self-esteem. Depression reigned yet again. My stressors swayed between my daughter and the bank—both seemed to be behaving with equally irrational intent. In addition, my three-year relationship came to an end. It seemed as though the planets were aligned—and not in my favour.

In an attempt to divert my daughter from her more worrying pursuits, I moved out of the city to my canal front home at Scarborough. Things grew steadily worse. I knew I had lost the plot when the highlight of my day was watching 'The Bold and the Beautiful'. I filled in the rest of the time by cooking muffins—and eating them. Unfortunately, they were very good muffins and my weight ballooned to ninety kilos. During this time, I had enough cash flow to not have to worry about ongoing work however, by not taking care of my finances and spending my days drifting from one negative thought to the next, my business suffered. I forgot to pay bills and do my tax, leading to obvious problems which later took quite some effort to rectify.

After a five-year muffin-eating hiatus, I decided it was time to put the negativity to one side and get back to living life, as I had done so many times previously. I had been living an unstructured life and surviving off my rental income but I now felt I needed some structure and discipline. I had not worked nine to five for a very long time. As the office mezzanine level of my commercial building was not in use, I decided to set up an office there. My daughter was now showing signs of exiting the rebellious phase and I was able to use this opportunity to work with her and mentor her in my business. She proved to be an excellent student and quickly learnt the various intricacies of the business. She was now a large part of my motivation to reinvent myself yet again and move on to bigger and better things. Together, we launched a new facet of my business, 'Keeping on Track™'. Through this business,

I had a vision of being able to do something to help other people overcome the challenges they face in life. I had experienced enough challenges of my own to know how necessary this is. My motivation was to create a forum for people to come together, share, collaborate and transform their life into something more fulfilling.

True to my life story, this was not to eventuate without difficulty.

My first big challenge in 'Keeping on Track™' was the 2011 floods. I had been on holiday and returned to find the building had been severely affected by floodwaters. I remember that particular morning my sister contacted me and warned me that there was a flood. As I had never been through a flood before, I had no idea of the severity of the situation or the impact it may have so I merely replied, "Yeah, I've got to go now" and thought nothing more of it.

This is a stunning building situated in Milton just off the popular coffee and restaurant strip at Park Road. Had I checked when buying I would have known that it was situated in a flood prone area; more evidence of the need for greater due diligence. Had I been aware of this, I could at least have had the building insured for 'disturbance of business' and 'loss of income'. I had two other properties badly affected by the floods, so organising renovations for all of them took quite a bit of effort and made for some anxious times and financially debilitating times.

Part 2 – Re-enter the Shadow

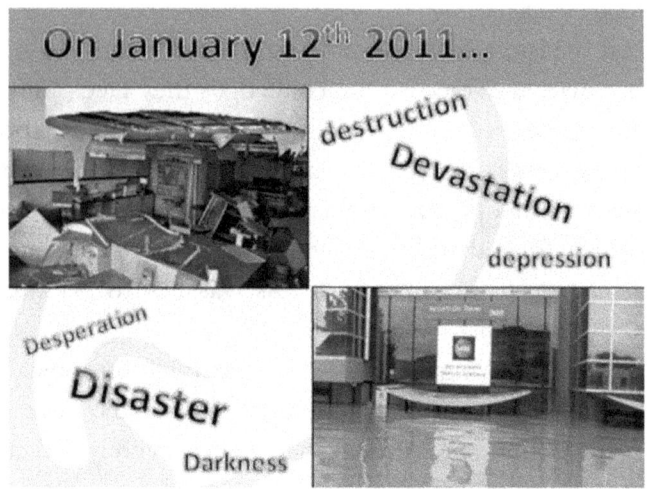

The Brisbane Floods 2011

While dealing with the aftermath of the flood was a horrific experience, I am now appreciative of the lessons I learnt from it. While this event had the usual ring of misfortune, it proved to be different in that I didn't fall apart by focusing on the negative. To the contrary, this time I could see the devastating effect the floods had on many people around me and because of that, I was able to focus outside of myself and draw on the positive. I feel this was a major step in shifting my mindset and helping me see a bigger picture. The property had a tenant with a ten-year lease but as he was suffering significant financial hardship due to loss of business after the floods, I released him from his contract. The floods had such a profoundly negative affect on so many people, and due to the fact leasing out the property had become impossible, I decided to use this adversity as an opportunity to reinvent myself. I decided to use the property to try and turn some of the misfortune into opportunity. As the property was not insured, I had to spend $100,000 of my own money refurbishing the property and I opened the property for meetings and workshops for women. This venture was called Meetings at Milton.

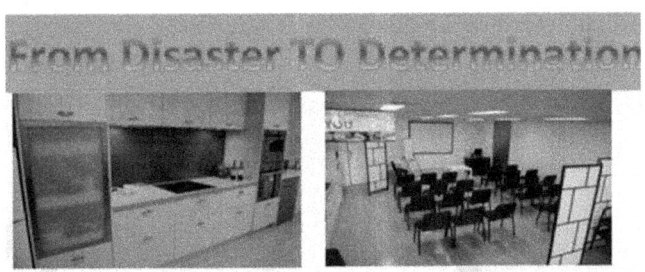

Orane transformed this adversity into an opportunity

Meetings at Milton

I did this for two reasons; to create a place where I could provide some sort of assistance for women experiencing various difficulties in their lives and also to help offset some of the income I was losing due to my tenants vacating the property in the wake of the floods.

I ran these meetings for a year and thoroughly enjoyed the experience of meeting, communicating and getting to know the many women who participated in the meetings and workshops. An international public speaker, Eric Bailey, agreed to collaborate with me for one event.

For me, this was a real growth experience as through it I learnt that I could do something I had previously been afraid of. I did it for a reason other than for myself but the result was that I benefited. I learnt a lot from the meetings and I hope the women that attended learnt something from me, the presenters and the other attendees. The hours were very long and I eventually found that I could not keep up the pace and attend to my other business commitments as well, so the meetings were discontinued. I rented the building out once again and returned full time to my passion, which was investing in property.

With guest speaker Eric Bailey

I now felt the time was right to extend my property holdings at Milton, so I began planning to build a duplex at the rear of my property. As I owned the land this would be a low-impact project as all I had to do is liaise with the builder and choose colours, fittings etc.

for the interior. Even though the market was rather flat, I still thought the time was right to begin this project.

Front view of property development in Milton

Rear view of property development in Milton

Once again, I decided to joint venture with a friend. As I have come to learn, sometimes through bitter experience, it is sensible to put certain precautions in place prior to beginning a project. We took legal advice on how to structure our agreement should one of us should not be able to complete the project for any reason such as death or incapacity, and we built in an exit strategy to accommodate such an eventuality.

My friend put in $550,000 and I put in the land. At the time of writing, this project is ongoing. We work on the project together and we will each benefit from the experience. During the project, my friend is able to gain experience in managing a project such as this and learning first-hand how to deal with the myriad of decisions that need to be made.

At the completion of the project, she will own a four-bedroom townhouse two kilometres from the city. I will also have a townhouse for minimal expense, which will create cash flow as well as giving me a freehold property.

Speaking at Meetings at Milton

Bring on the fifties

"Often, it's not about becoming a new person, but becoming the person you were meant to be, and already are, but don't know how to be."

Heath L Buckmaster

I was approaching my fiftieth birthday when I was sitting on that plane from Launceston. Although I had achieved so much in my life, I still didn't feel happy, I didn't feel fulfilled. I still felt that if that 'black dog' came knocking, I would open the door and let him in. I had achieved so much in my life and I needed to understand why I still felt there was something missing.

My children were now in the process of creating their own lives and engineering their own future success stories. I also had to accept that I was reaching retirement age and I felt the need to reinvent myself and find my purpose. Planning retirement is a crucial part of thriving and surviving but, I believe, has been a much bigger challenge for Baby Boomers than previous generations. Due to the volatility of social as well as employment factors impacting my generation, planning has, for many people, been a stab in the dark. Changes in technology, government incentives and world economics have made planning for retirement a speciality that not everyone could understand in a manner necessary for effective planning. In general figures, a woman who is fifty-five years old today can expect to live to eighty-nine years of age and a man of fifty-five has a life expectancy of eighty-two years, however there will be many people who outlive the forecasted expectancy and who need to retain a meaningful place in our society and be able to live with dignity and grace. The effect this will have on individual retirement planning as well as its overall impact on society in general cannot be understated. The estimates relating to the number of Baby Boomers who will not be able to live in comfortable retirement are varied but always unsettling. One estimate suggests that eighty percent of Baby Boomers will not be able to afford a comfortable retirement.

The need to create additional wealth for retirement is now more obvious than ever but not as unachievable as one may first think. The identifiable mark of a Baby Boomer is—in the words of Frank Sinatra—a determination to do it their way and this mindset is what will help them to continue to rewrite the book.

I started to go through menopause. I found that I longed for time alone, I longed for a sanctuary that offered me calm and harmony. I wanted freedom from distractions and demands of other people; I wanted to insulate myself from noise and telephones. I was starting to reflect on my past, I felt the need to resolve unfinished business from my past.

Facing menopause necessitates regrouping and rethinking. It's a rite of passage that, while taking some effort and expertise to negotiate, acts as a catalyst for change. Personally, after I accepted the idea I found it exhilarating. It was like throwing off an old worn out coat and feeling the winds of freedom buffet and chill me through to my bones. The chill energised me and the wind destabilised me with its energy, but it was all good. I felt alive and I felt empowered; able to pull all the entangled strings of the fragments of my past together and to weave the fabric for a life that I had been trying to piece together for so long. The part of me I knew existed but could never quite capture began to emerge and I felt increasingly comfortable with the new me. I even liked the new me. I was smarter than I had previously thought. I realised that I had indeed accomplished past achievements because I had the ability to do so and not just because I was lucky or because someone else helped me.

For the first time, I was able to pause for breath and look around me. What had struck me like a bolt of lightning while being involved in the workshops for women was; I was not alone. If depression is one thing, it is isolating. You don't contemplate suicide when you feel welcomed as part of a family, group or society in general. Depression makes you feel like it's you alone against the world, and sometimes that is the way it is or at least that is the way we make it, albeit unknowingly. I had spent so much of my life since early childhood feeling alone and isolated, often believing there must be a reason for my situation but never being able to comprehend it. I think those miserable school days when I was made to sit outside in the sun with a sign on my back damning me to an intellectual hell, laid the foundation for me to feel isolated and alone even when part of a group, family or community.

I felt a fundamental change happening that brought with it a distinctive empowerment and I recognised it as the beginning of the rainbow that I had been chasing for a very long time.

Today, five years on from that plane journey, I am stable in all aspects of my life. I have found strategies to overcome my depression. I have found peace and happiness from the inside. My focus now is to make a difference to other people's lives. I want to share my experiences with others, to speak openly about my challenges, and to provide an example to others who are similar, or even worse, situations. I want to inspire women to take their lives to the next level, there is hope for all of us and I want to help other women to achieve their dreams.

The next chapter is just beginning; I am looking forward to the rest of my life.

Part 3

My journey

"You gain strength, courage and confidence by every experience in which you really stop to look fear in the face. You must do the thing you think you cannot do."

Eleanor Roosevelt

For me, the flowers began to bloom at the age of fifty, after thirty-five years of searching. It's been a long bumpy ride and as I look back, I cannot but feel sorrow for all the damage I have caused along the way. I allowed the shadow side of my personality to dominate me and my loved ones again and again despite my efforts to the contrary. Self-gratification was my desired destination on a journey fuelled by ego, but it was a destination never to be reached. Just when I thought I had the horizon in view, a disaster would strike, and pull me down into a hole that I could not climb out of by myself; nor would I allow anyone else to help me. So there I would sit, sometimes for years, wallowing in my misery and doing my best to make all those around me suffer as well.

From the time of my divorce, I laboured, at times to the point of obsession, to find an easier path. I studied a seemingly endless number of self-help books and listened to whichever guru was making headlines at the time in an effort to become a better version of me.

Many times, I tried to become someone else entirely and that was usually when things went horribly wrong. It was a long, slow, winding road that brought me to where I am now with the sacrifices demanded by this journey sometimes severe, and so it is with most people. I believe the human experience transcends gender, social and economic status, ethnicity, and age leaving each of us prone to the same human emotional frailties and, by extension, a shared responsibility to help each other whenever and however possible.

My single most challenging obstacle needing to be overcome along the way has been fear. Fear is a devious component of our emotional make-up. It lurks deep in the shadows of our psyche and masquerades as aspects of our whole that would appear to be totally unrelated. Fear often leads to negative compensatory behaviour. When I think back on my life, it was fear of losing my children that drove me to work long hours and develop all sorts of strategies to beat the competition. It was fear of losing my partner that drove me to constantly analyse our relationship and make excessive demands of him to prove his loyalty and love to me. It was fear for my own sanity that drove me further into depression.

Of all the faces of fear, the one that has dogged me the most is fear of failure. The bravado with which I attempted many challenges in my life was in reality, an attempt to kill the fear. I felt that if I could control the fear I could control my future. For me, fear and control have been different sides of the same coin. What I most feared losing; I tried to control, and due to the extreme methods I employed often lost the object of my need. Today, I am most grateful that I still have my family; with them, I have a full life and a positive outlook for our future.

To advance beyond fear requires change, and for those people shrouded in a blanket of fear, change has the magnitude of Mount Everest. For me, it didn't matter how much I read, thought and planned, taking that first step upwards was always difficult. I guess it's a bit like giving up smoking. First, you tell yourself it is okay to smoke; many people do it without negative consequences. Then you think you can give up at any time if you really want to—but not at the moment. Then you try and fail. Then you find an excuse for the failure based on factors other than the lack of your own willpower. Then you try again and fail for the same reason. Then you think it doesn't matter, smoking isn't all that bad. Then, if you are really committed to change, you get help.

Fear of change is a normal human reaction when security is threatened and for some people, any change is a threat to their security. I see personal change as being like the ocean. Sometimes it is calm and moves gently to and fro causing minimal disturbance but at other times, it is turbulent, tossing and turning itself inside out and destroying all in its path. This is the nature of change.

Taking action to implement personal change in the face of fear takes courage, and during those times when change is most needed, courage is often in short supply. The challenge is to seek it, find it and use it, to tap into the currents of the ocean and navigate them to your advantage, taking you from fear to faith. The words of Nelson Mandela often encouraged me when I felt afraid, **"Courage is not the absence of fear, but the triumph over it"**. Faith is the reward of change—faith in one's own ability to change, survive and thrive. For me, faith in myself led to the development of self-esteem based on who I am and what I do rather than the external factors of physical appearance, material wealth and the recognition from others based on their own criteria.

As creatures of habit, we tend to return again and again to the behaviours that served us so poorly; and I did just that. I continually focused on the external rather than the internal. My obsession with the external: good looks, expensive cars and showy houses fed my external self as I laboured to portray myself as a successful businesswoman who had it all under control. However, the reality was very different. At the same time, my internal self cried out for recognition of the real me; the me that walked every inch of every mile in emotional chaos, with every step reinforcing my all-encompassing feelings of failure.

When I think of the Orane I knew in the past I see a woman who became upset when things didn't go her way, a woman who wallowed in self-pity and blamed others for her misery, using intimidation and coercion to achieve and satisfy her wants. A woman who experienced constant conflict in her personal relationships and who wavered wildly between her need and neglect of others. A woman with little self-discipline, addicted to the adrenalin rush supplied by nervous energy and risk taking. In my mind, I see the image of an Orane I once knew, but with whom I am no longer familiar.

I had to learn what it was that I needed to make me happy just as a young child, as part of its development toward adulthood learns, one lesson at a time, how to separate the ego from the self. I had to take myself back to my 'emotional childhood' and grow anew.

After much serious soul-searching over an extended period of time and with considerable effort, these were the things that I identified as important; the goals that I set for myself.

1. To find strategies to overcome my depression
2. To gain the self-confidence and self-esteem that I had yearned for
3. To never be financially dependent on a man
4. To never be dependent on a government pension
5. To have dignity in old age and be comfortable instead of struggling
6. To be able to pass this wealth down to the next generation and finally break of the shackles of poverty inherited by my ancestors
7. To live from the income of my personal resources and not be shackled to a nine to five job.
8. To make a difference by sharing the lessons I have learnt and the strategies to get you from where you are to where you want to be.

For many years, I was in denial about the fact that I was depressed. When I finally developed the courage to get out of denial, I made a decision—I was going to do whatever was necessary to overcome this impediment.

I did a lot of research about my condition and realised if I wanted to overcome the depression, I was going to have to change my lifestyle. I stopped smoking, I stopped drinking alcohol and coffee, and cut out sugar. I started exercising every day, as I understood that physical activity counteracts a predisposition to anxiety and helps relieve depression. I was very disciplined, I focussed on the results and did not allow myself to make excuses or give up the regime.

I also realised that I suffered from hypoglycaemia, a condition where your blood sugar drops very rapidly which has been known to aggravate anxiety. After an allergy test, I was diagnosed as having allergies to certain foods. In hindsight, I believe this was the cause of a lot of my earlier problems; my symptoms were depression, mood swings, irritability and insomnia. Therefore, I had to eliminate a lot of foods from my diet.

In looking back over my life, I was able to identify certain common factors relating to my episodes of depression. I started to understand the triggers for my episodes of depression. Prior to each downward spiral, I experienced a time of particularly severe turmoil, which left me feeling bereft of direction and unable to move forward towards my goals. The particular crisis may have been material, as in the case of my losing my job in Sydney due to the closure of the company, or it may have been emotional as in the case of my divorce. Some life event would act as a trigger, and due to my lack of resources, I would descend into depression. I believe there are two overriding factors that contributed to this recurring behaviour: firstly, my mother's usual response to the challenges she faced in her life which was imprinted on my mind at a young age and secondly, the fact that I had not developed sufficiently sound strategies to deal with disappointment and stress in adulthood. When some event in my life caused friction or turmoil I responded in like and began on the slippery path of descent. Given my life-long focus on all things external, it is not surprising that I had fallen somewhat short on developing useful life strategies for dealing with the unknown and unwanted. Understanding the triggers helped greatly in my battle against depression. By knowing the triggers and the early signs, I could develop strategies to prevent a relapse.

I changed my mindset. I learnt how to use my creativity to distract me when I felt myself drawn to that dark place that I knew only too well. Instead of succumbing, I would go to the kitchen and bake a cake or make a delicious meal for the children.

Most importantly, I started investing in myself. I started to read books and listen to tapes to build my self-esteem and my confidence and create a life of spiritual orientation.

I believe the essential components to a successful life are confidence and self-esteem. Developing those attributes were my first big steps on the road to success.

After I gained confidence in myself—which took years of work—I started to appreciate myself more and as I did so I began to see life events with greater clarity. With the clarity emerged a vision of what I wanted, after which I could plan what I was prepared to give up in order to achieve my goals.

I set out a plan of action, a road map, and did not deviate from it. I became self-disciplined and developed the ability to do what I knew I should do and when I should do it, whether I liked it or not. Once clear about what I wanted I was able to make the right choices in life. I chose people who would guide and support and inspire me. I waved goodbye to the dream-stealers and eliminated toxic, negative people from my life.

The one constant that does appear as a common thread throughout my life is the reliance on property to heal the financial and emotional wounds. Once back on track, I would again dive into the property market with all the hunger of a bear coming out of hibernation and looking for its first meal. I chose properties to which I could add value and thereby increase my property portfolio and income.

Property has been a lifelong interest handed down to me from my parents from those early days when they would build one house, sell it and build again. It has been my financial and emotional saviour on many occasions, an outlet for my creativity and my retirement plan for the future.

Lessons I have learnt

"Above all, be the heroine of your life, not the victim."

Nora Ephron

I have learnt many lessons in my journey in life and I want to share these with you. My hope is that it will help you avoid making some of the mistakes that I have, and in turn avoid the pain and suffering that accompanies such mistakes. I hope to inspire you to take control of your life by identifying the barriers that stand between you and your goals. I want to help you fight that devious enemy 'fear of failure' that holds so many people hostage. I hope that by sharing these lessons, it will give you the confidence and the courage to chase your dreams and turn them into reality.

Take action

"Let us not look back in anger, nor forward in fear, but around in awareness"

James Thurber

First and foremost, you need to recognise that there is a need for change.

You need to look inside yourself and understand what it is that you are looking for. You cannot be satisfied when nothing of substance and longevity can be attained in the outside world, nothing worth as much as those inner treasures within yourself. So close your eyes and listen to your inner voice. If you are patient (it does take time) and you go on looking inside, you will start to understand what it is that you are searching for.

Formulate a clear concept of what it is that will make you happy; you must define it. Unless you know what you are seeking, how will you find it?

Once you know who you are, what you want and where you are going, nothing can stop you.

Become educated

"You have to go wholeheartedly into anything in order to achieve anything worth having."

Frank Lloyd Wright

We all have a passion; my passion was property. I had always used property as an escape and it was the thing that I always turned to when I needed to pull myself out of the hole. We need to identify what it is that we are passionate about and start doing it, or improve on how we do it.

There is always more to learn and to learn more improves the chances of living life to the full. I educated myself about property and although I learnt many things the hard way, I stuck with it until I learnt enough to make me relatively wealthy. I did this against the odds; by the time I became an adult I was quite convinced that I had a learning disorder due to my childhood school experiences. I could have let those negative experiences dictate my life, but I worked hard and never gave up learning about the thing that fascinated me the most and that is property. I read books, listened to other people's experiences, both good and bad. I kept up with trends in the property market and asked lots of questions. I was never afraid to try something new even though I did not have the qualifications or experience to do it. I had no formal learning or training to rely on, so I relied on myself and for this reason, perhaps my intuition developed well and stood me in good stead when I had nothing more concrete. I truly believe that when the student is ready, the teacher will appear and to this end I always tried to keep an open mind in relation to how that would transpire. I have learnt some of my most valuable lessons from the most discouraging and sometimes inhospitable people and situations.

Find a mentor

"Mentoring is a brain to pick, an ear to listen, and a push in the right direction."

John C Crosby

Find a mentor who will encourage and motivate you to achieve your goals.

A mentor is more than a trainer or expert in the field; they are interested in you as a person and want to help you reach your goals. A mentor will provide you with the scope to create a dream and the tools to make it happen.

Create a life of quality

"The quality, not the longevity of one's life is what is important."

Martin Luther King, Jr

This lesson I learnt from my mother and it is in no way related to money, as my parents had very little. It was more a way of life that I later, upon reflection, identified as a lesson I learnt very early and one that has stood me in good stead during dark times. My mother is a wonderful cook and always provided her family with beautiful food, which was enjoyed in an atmosphere of appreciation, not only for the food, but the way in which it was presented. My mother's table was always arranged with care and she insisted our family sit and eat with dignity. My siblings and I were taught from a very early age that to sit at a table and eat, required good manners and that appreciation for the food and the effort that went into preparing it was part of the dining experience, regardless of our financial situation. For this lesson, I am also forever grateful, as I have passed these culinary skills and the 'culture of appreciation' onto my children.

Even during my dark days of depression, when I felt hopeless and worthless, I could manage to prepare good food and share it with my family in a way that made all seem right with the world, even just momentarily. At certain times during my life, cooking was the only creative outlet I had and I believe it is necessary that we each have one form of creativity that we can fall back on when life isn't unfolding as planned. This provides an outlet for otherwise stifled emotions, as well as allowing us to step back and appreciate something we have done that has merit.

Creativity creates wealth

"All the breaks you need in life wait within your imagination. Imagination is the workshop of your mind, capable of turning mind energy into accomplishment and wealth."

Napoleon Hill

Giving yourself permission to be creative in any field has ongoing benefit; when creativity flourishes in one form it will flourish in another. The brain cannot be turned off easily when it's on a roll; keep it going and anything is possible, as recent research in brain plasticity shows only too clearly. The 1940s writer Napoleon Hill understood the importance of creativity linked with positivity and his writing provided the roadmap for many later works relating to the development of wealth through positive thinking.

"Life is not about finding yourself. Life is about creating yourself."

George Bernard Shaw

These words echo in my mind constantly: For me, this is one of life's truisms. Nothing eventuates without some form of creativity and to squash creativity is to disengage from life. While creativity is the bedrock of any successful endeavour, it is not something that simply appears out of the blue. Creativity has to be developed and nurtured. Creativity needs time and commitment and it also needs forgiveness because it's not easy to get things right the first time. It was a breakthrough moment for me when I realised that I had been implementing creative strategies in various aspects of my life without being aware of it. While the formal side of my academic development was lacking the creative side has always been in high gear. Now I understand that, I appreciate it and use it with greater skill.

Understand your core values

"Your vision will become clear only when you look into your heart. Who looks outside, dreams. Who looks inside, awakens."

Carl Jung

Understanding your core values is central to understanding yourself. Without this knowledge, it is easy to be rocked by the opinions of others or the turbulent twists and turns of life. Without our core values we cannot know who we are or why we act the way we do. We do not understand the boundaries we have set for ourselves, or indeed, if we have solid boundaries at all.

Our core values reflect our belief systems and provide a basis for self-respect and continued growth. When I think of what brings value into my life and what I need to align with my core values they are my family, freedom, personal growth, making a difference and taking a risk.

My family

They are the wind beneath my wings and give me the courage to carry on when the road is long and winding. They give me a sense of belonging when challenges occur and being with them makes all right in the world. My life story depicts the turbulent times we have endured as a family, from my primary family comprising my parents and eight children to my present family, myself and my four children. Families are fluid and what seems solid today may be very shaky tomorrow. Family life demands flexibility on many fronts and this is not always easy to accommodate. My family suffered greatly due to my depression and it is to them I owe my present well-being.

Freedom

For me this is being able to do what I want, when I want, for as long as I want, with whom I want, and not having to ask permission to do so. It is a licence to be me. My early childhood was a difficult time of fruitless attempts to fit into the norm. I attempted to grow up in a shell provided by other people, fitting other people's specifications. I didn't fit. I tried to be what my classroom teachers expected of me based on the abilities of other children, but I couldn't. I tried to be what my husband wanted, but his choices told me I didn't shape up. I tried to be what I wanted, but I could never live up to that either. Then I learnt how to redefine my goals. I made an effort to give up blaming and start taking responsibility for my life. I decided that when I woke up each morning it was my choice as to whether it would be a good day or a bad day. I decided to start thinking about other people and how I could be of service to them rather than focusing solely on myself. Freedom came from taking responsibility for myself.

Personal growth

Personal growth is about viewing myself as an asset and being able to invest in that asset to the extent that I believe is beneficial and enjoyable. It's feeling good about myself and my journey and taking responsibility for that journey. It's about not being anchored in the past and re-enacting the bad times, it's about letting go of the negative and embracing the positive, however and whatever that may entail. It's also about being content with what I feel is worthwhile and not chasing someone else's dream. I have also learnt that it's about caring for other people and learning to understand that they also have needs that I have a responsibility to meet.

Making a difference

I believe that as we all cohabit this planet, we each subscribe to an unwritten universal law to look after it and each other. Without this collective responsibility, we are nothing more than disconnected entities spinning in our own circles and this, I believe, is why we often drift without direction. I see an increased awareness by entrepreneurs and businesses of the need for a social conscience and this is something I continually strive to incorporate in my business endeavours. This is a work in progress and something I am always on the lookout to improve.

Taking a risk

Many people avoid risk in an effort to avoid pain and suffering however, I believe that pain and suffering have their own benefits, which include learning how to change and relearn new things, learning how to love and grow, and learning how to reach full potential. While taking risks has led me into some very difficult situations it has also been the catalyst for my growth, change and independence. I believe a person who risks nothing, achieves nothing. While my journey has involved taking significant personal and financial risks, I hope, through my own experience, to provide guidance for others that may involve less risk to them while still being able to achieve an acceptable outcome.

Property

"To lose yourself in something you love is to find yourself."

Tod Siler

When buying real estate, confidence in yourself is your fundamental power. You need to have real clarity about the what, where, when and how much you need to pay. And most importantly, you need to know how you can add value. Armed with this information, you can take calculated risks and will make the right choices.

Creative flair enables you to purchase property, renovate, add value, transform a block of land into a development site, sub-divide, and strata title. You become a visionary.

You need to have the ability to communicate in a positive way. Words nourish your brain or deplete it; they can be your greatest asset or your greatest liability. You need to be able to communicate with confidence with bankers to attain the correct loan so that it can be utilised appropriately in the future.

Do not cross collateralise your property through ignorance as this could cause distress down the track.

Collaborate with your team of experts e.g. lawyers, accountants, architects, bankers and town planners and use their skills as leverage to take you to the next level and increase your wealth and cash flow. Collaboration with others may even include using someone else's money and your skill. For example, I once purchased a development site with a friend, he put his house up as security, I proceeded to use my skills and his money to get a Development Approval, and we now own the development site with approval for 12 waterfront luxury units.

The confident, educated investor does not solely rely on capital growth, nor are they concerned whether the property market booms or busts. They create cash flow that continues to increase and they live from the income of their personal resources. This is how I took my life from fear to financial freedom. I have total control over my life. I am not shackled to a job, or dependent on social security.

My future

"Contentment is not the fulfilment of what you want, but the realisation of how much you already have."

Anonymous

Struggle has been a large, essential part of my life. Without the struggle, there would have been no vision and without a vision, there would have been no change and no future. The struggles I experienced afforded me the opportunity to develop the courage I needed to heal my wounds and mould a better, more positive future. I spent a lot of time in my early life wondering what the purpose was for my being here, or indeed, if there was a purpose at all. I now believe that the purpose only begins to manifest itself after one has made enough mistakes and learnt enough lessons to create a platform upon which the purpose can grow. For some people this can be a relatively quick process but for others, such as myself, it has been lengthy.

My ego has a lot to answer for as it was my ego that sabotaged much of my progress and kept me embalmed in the rotted bindings of shame and pessimism. My ego closed my mind to the teachers who appeared in my life, leaving me bereft of the knowledge so sorely needed and having to learn the same lesson yet again. Ego kept me a victim and gave me the go-ahead to blame everyone else rather than take responsibility for my own actions and decisions. Ego is still a demon that I fight to keep under control as to let it loose will mean havoc for myself and those I value.

Ego is a fellow comrade of fear; it lays dormant and then unexpectedly surfaces, doing its damage and retreating before it can even be identified. The aim is destabilisation and fragmentation. Empowerment and self-esteem are the archenemies of ego and fear because they work within limits and respect other players in the game. They use personal responsibility as a springboard to do their work and don't play on the vulnerable. I take care of the empowerment and self-esteem I have developed as I know they are working for me and not against me, they will lead me into the future.

The teachers I now accept into my life prove to be mentors, giving guidance and encouragement when I need it most. It is through accepting the guidance and support of others, often offered freely, that I have been able to pull myself out of the confines of depression and create a more meaningful life.

For me, hardship has been a relentless but effective taskmaster. Surviving my experiences has brought real clarity to me; clarity that I would like the opportunity to share with other people, to help them on their journey and to help them avoid the pitfalls I have fallen victim to. I want to share the answers I've discovered and lay them on the table of experience for others to taste and come back for more if they find them to their liking. I want other people to ponder some of my experiences, my lessons and my approach to life because in so doing they just may find some direction for their own journey.

We all face multiple hardships throughout our life; some self-inflicted and others due to the dubious generosity of other people or fate. I believe we each have a duty of care to help and guide each other through life if at all possible, to the betterment of our individual lives and to the betterment of us as a species here on this planet we inhabit. I believe we each have a uniqueness that is inherently valuable and when shared will be of greater value. I plan to provide a forum for this to eventuate and it is my sincere wish that you and others join me in helping, even a little, people who need support in finding their way to a healthier emotional and financial future. I am currently developing a personal development program through 'Keeping on Track™', which will be a resource to help people transform their life and achieve their highest potential.

Your Key from Fear to Financial Freedom

"When you are inspired by some great purpose, some extraordinary project, all your thoughts break their bonds. Your mind transcends limitations, your consciousness expands in every direction and you find yourself in a new, great and wonderful world."

Patanjali

I transformed my life to become a self-made millionaire in the space of three years, due to sheer determination to lift myself out of the poverty mentality passed down through generations. I have overcome misfortune and used the low points in my life as opportunities to learn and grow, using my passion for property as a vehicle for financial success.

I know that life is about choices, but I didn't realise how significant the impact of our choices can have on our lives and how I could create an amazing life for myself just by making some different choices.

The secret? There is no secret. By getting my life on track, I readily received these long lost answers to the questions that haunted me and held me back for so long.

I'd like to share the answers I've discovered. I'd like you to ponder some of my experiences, my lessons and my approach to life. My purpose is to help those that are facing hardships. Not to commiserate but to show you that there *are* answers, there *are* ways to overcome your hardships. There is a way to get back on track.

I have a genuine passion for helping people get back on track. That's why I'm here and that's why I started Keeping on Track™.

Keeping on Track™ is your key from fear to financial freedom. I want to help you learn how you can transform your life and gain emotional and financial freedom.

As part of Keeping on Track™, I am developing programs to help people transform their lives into the lives they want to lead. Within all of us, we have dreams, and we have barriers and concerns that prevent us achieving our dreams. We all have values and things that are important in our lives. We all have a passion, something that we love doing. Sometimes, all these things are not immediately obvious, but within each of us, we have the answers to a happier and more fulfilling life; our programs helps you find these answers. All you need to have is the commitment and enthusiasm to transform your life.

I am developing a seven-step program to help you find the answers. **Confidence** is your fundamental power. The quality of your health, wealth, relationship and career completely revolves and emerges from your understanding of self-esteem. With healthy self-esteem, you develop **confidence,** which enables you to see life with **clarity** and make the right **choices** in life. **Creativity** is also an intrinsic power in your life; through it you will find your passion and create wealth. Live it, breathe it, think it, ink it, master it. With the strategies you will learn, **communication** with yourself and with others will improve dramatically. You will learn how to **collaborate** with other people and use it as leverage to take your life to a different level. You will learn strategies to create **cashflow** through your passion, your business, your property or your career.

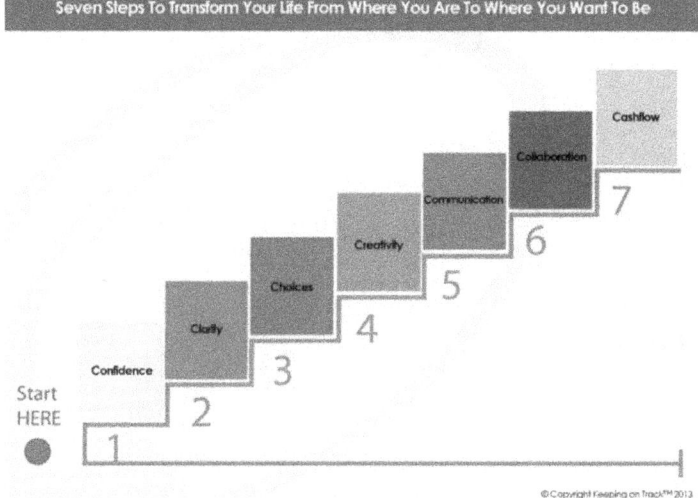

When you transform yourself, you transform everything about your life.

Visit **www.keepingontrack.com.au** to find out how you can transform your life. You can read our articles, sign up to our newsletter and find out the latest developments with 'Keeping on Track™'.

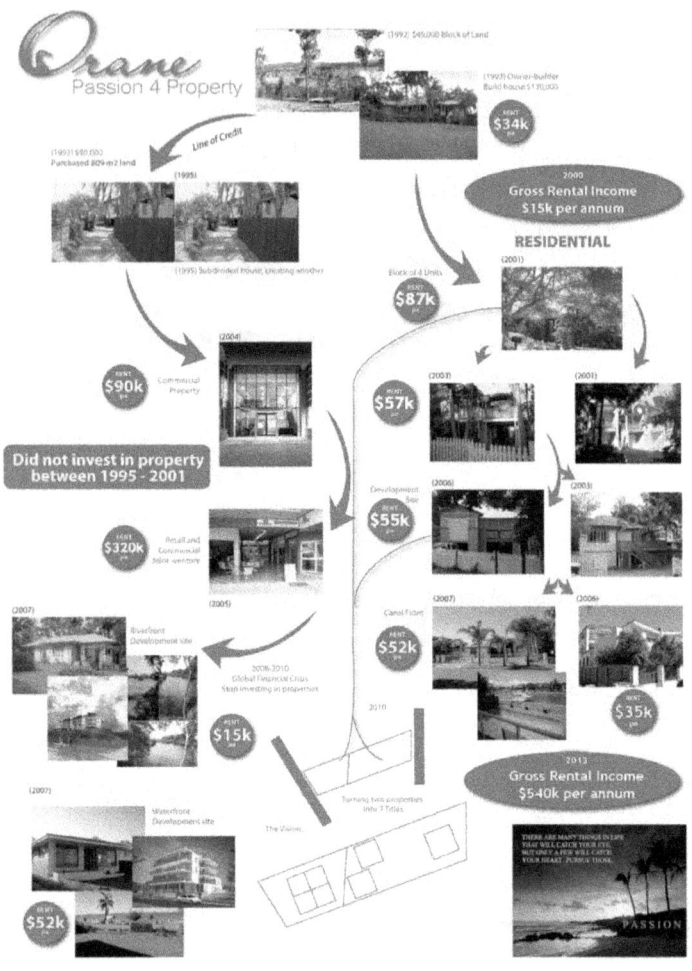

My journey from fear to financial freedom

"There are many things in life that will catch your eye, but only a few will catch your heart…pursue those."

Michael Nolan

About The Author

Orane Swan has a proven track record, she is passionate, persistent, proactive, professional and prosperous. This single mother of four children with no formal qualifications relentlessly pursued her passions, whilst dealing with life's stresses and struggles and became a self-made millionaire.

"I've had an amazing life. Full of pain, loss, setbacks, rejection, ill health and poverty as well as prosperity when I got my life back on track. For all these things, I am most grateful. I also know that life is about choices and when that happened, I realised that I could make some different choices and create an even more amazing life."

Orane spent the first half of her life coming to terms with debilitating adversities and building a life of financial prosperity, mental stability, and spiritual orientation.

Like many stories of adversity, her achievements were earned through self-discipline and a complete rethink of how she—and her children—were going to survive. This didn't happen over the course of a weekend seminar or reading a book, it took many years.

"Hardship has been an effective task-master. Surviving these experiences has brought real clarity. And I want to share with you, what I found to be the key to finding these answers."

Orane's transformation from no self-esteem to high self-esteem wasn't due to financial success. Rather, her amazing financial success was the result of her inner-transformation. And herein lays the core of her desire, passion, and mission, to share with others that they too can be transformed.

Orane is available to speak at your event, seminar or workshop. Visit **www.keepingontrack.com.au** for more information.

"Every woman that finally figured out her worth has picked up her suitcases of pride and boarded a flight to freedom, which landed in the valley of change."

Shannon L. Alder

www.ingramcontent.com/pod-product-compliance
Lightning Source LLC
Chambersburg PA
CBHW070051120426
42742CB00048B/2397